HANS URS VON BALTHASAR

HEART OF THE WORLD

HANS URS VON BALTHASAR

HEART OF THE WORLD

TRANSLATED BY ERASMO S. LEIVA

IGNATIUS PRESS SAN FRANCISCO

Title of the German original:
Das Herz der Welt
© 1954 by Peter Shifferli
Arche Verlag, Zürich

Cover by Victoria Hoke Lane

Published with ecclesiastical approval
© 1979 by Ignatius Press, San Francisco
All rights reserved
ISBN 978-0-89870-001-5
Library of Congress Control Number 79-84879
Printed in the United States of America ∞

CONTENTS

Translator's note   7

Preface   13

PART ONE: THE KINGDOM

I   The Flowing Stream   19
II   The Coming of the Light   37
III   The Broken Sun   58
IV   The Father's Vineyard   73

PART TWO: THE SUFFERING

V   The Putting-off Game   91
VI   The Eye of the Peacock   104
VII   The Intruder   117
VIII   Jailhouse and Cocoon   133
IX   A Wound Has Blossomed   145

PART THREE: THE VICTORY

X   Rose of Sorrows   157
XI   And the Sea of Being Lay Dry   174
XII   The Conquest of the Bride   189
XIII   Love—a Wilderness   204

This little volume will come as a surprise even to av-
id readers of Father von Balthasar's other translated
works. The religious ardor of the poet-theologian usu-
ally evades us with all the pure serenity of a volcano
under snow. But in revealing to us the Heart of the
World he could not do less than bare his own heart.
The poetic form of the work, in particular, strikes us
with its intimate tone.

Everywhere in the extensive corpus of his writings
we are accustomed to finding that happy union between beauty of expression and profundity of content
that characterizes his theology. In this he follows a
principle he has himself elaborated elsewhere: that a
beautiful object ought not to be spoken about in any
but a beautiful manner.

Who could hesitate to say that the constant theme of
Balthasar's theology is the abyss of God's love? And
what other subject, by its native beauty, could prove a
greater challenge to aesthetic creativity? But nowhere
does he explore the unifying might of faith with more
urgency than in *Heart of the World*, for here we cannot

escape the stern beauty of that Face whose every glance heals and saves.

The austere lyricism of these meditations is no external embellishment, added to the dogmatic substance so as to make it more enticing. Perhaps the key to all of von Balthasar's work, and his principal contribution to modern Christian theology, is the rediscovery and practical application of an axiom unquestioned by either Scripture or the Fathers: the strict unity existing between the transcendental content and the perceivable form of revelation. God manifests his eternal love for us not *behind* the Scriptures, the sacraments, the magisterium, but *within* them. In the last analysis, if the beauty of Christian faith is an intrinsic and indispensable aspect of the divine economy, it is not because a certain (romanticizing) school of theology chooses to see it as such. It is because in this beauty we confront nothing other than the radiance of the incarnate Word himself.

And so, the vibrant christological poetry before us is the epiphany of a lively faith that issues from the depths of the experience of God, a faith that cannot help but sing in a music of image, surprise, color, movement. These poetic elements go to shape a breathless hymn of praise whose continual invention and variety witness to the infinite richness of the object in question: the human Heart of God. The lyrical form of this theology, then, is no personal whim of the author; its perfect pattern crystallizes in lucid obedience to the nature of his material.

Heart of the World deserves a place next to the *Imitation of Christ*. Especially in the passages where Christ speaks to the soul, Father von Balthasar shows himself a worthy successor of Thomas à Kempis. Both works combine an intense personal piety with a precise awareness of the believer's position as child and servant of Christ's Church. And if I add that they both speak "from the heart", I do not mean that they typify the tradition of subjective pietism, but that they are ruthlessly honest in not falsifying for a moment the anguish and the mortal risks which the disciple shares with the rest of men. For Balthasar, as for Kempis and all genuine Christians, the saint is first and foremost the one who renders constant thanks for having been loved and who never forgets the misery of once not having loved or let God love. The joy and the peace of Christ cannot be conjured up at will by an obsessive desire for happiness. They follow only from our deliverance out of a private abyss of illusion, and they are perfected by our groping attempt to be worthy of such a Lover: *Sic nos amantem quis non redamaret?*

Fully a master of linguistic audacity in the tradition of Goethe, Rilke and Heidegger, von Balthasar exploits the endless poetic resources of German syntax and word-construction. Often, to show hidden relationships among things, he can make a German root literally "blossom" by using it in several variations in rapid succession. Thus, we encounter a sentence such as this: *Jede Richtung ist ein Gericht und eine Hinrichtung, jede Ausführung ist eine Exekution, jede Weisung eine*

Verweisung (ch. 13), which a translator can attempt to reproduce with relative success with pairs such as execution/prosecution, prescription/proscription, etc. But when later in the same chapter we read: *Denn alles ist Rune, aber sie raunt von dir, und alles ist Zeichen und zeigt auf dich*, then the translator's inventiveness despairs and he must be content with a straightforward, lusterless rendering that cannot, alas, avoid dulling the sculptured edge of the original.

More than thirty years after its first appearance the book has lost none of its freshness of impact and hard truth. This, no doubt, is in great part due to its having been steeled in the furnace of the Second World War. I can think of no other work of spirituality which speaks more effectively and directly to the yearning of our distraught age for an integration of all aspects of human existence. Emotions, intellect and will are here shown vivified and redeemed in their common response to God's wooing for man's love.

In the original edition the chapters are untitled. The editor of this edition has judged it useful to introduce as headings phrases drawn from the text. Likewise, the original edition has no preface. The preface to the present edition, different in tone from the rest of the book, is in fact the section *"Das Offene Herz"* from Father von Balthasar's contribution to *Mysterium Salutis*, v. 3, part 2: *Das Christusereignis* (216–19), an exposition of the paschal mystery by leading theologians.

I am grateful to the International Institute of the Heart of Jesus for the gift that made possible this English version of *Das Herz der Welt* (3rd rev. ed.; Zürich: Verlag der Arche, 1945). Particular thanks go to Father Joseph Fessio, S. J., for his painstaking work in comparing first draft and original. The translation is dedicated to Mireya Letayf, my wife, *mujer de corazón*, and to John Galten, in friendship. These know the meaning of the poem by Angelus Silesius:

> *The light of divine glory*
>   *Shines in the breast of night:*
> *Who can see it? A heart*
>   *Whose eyes keep watch, e'er bright.*

ERASMO LEIVA

St. Ignatius Institute
University of San Francisco
Feast of Our Lady of Mount Carmel, 1979.

T HE VERY FORM OF THE CROSS, extending out into the four winds, always told the ancient Church that the Cross means solidarity: its outstretched arms would gladly embrace the universe. According to the *Didache*, the Cross is *sēmeion epektaseōs*, a "sign of expansion," and only God himself can have such a wide reach: "On the Cross God stretched out his hands to encompass the bounds of the universe" (Cyril of Jerusalem). "In his suffering God stretched out his arms and embraced the world, thus prefiguring the coming of a people which would, from East to West, gather under his wings" (Lactantius). "O blessed Wood on which God was stretched out!" (Sibylline Oracles). But God can do this only as a man, and his form is different from that of the animals in that "he can stand up straight and spread out his hands" (Justin). And thus it is that he can reach out to the two peoples, represented by the two thieves, and tear down the wall of division (Athanasius). Even in its outward form the Cross is all-inclusive.

But its interior inclusiveness is shown by the opened Heart out of which the last drops of Jesus'

13

substance are poured: blood and water, the sacraments of the Church. Both Biblically and philosophically (in the total human context, that is), the heart is conceived to be the real center of spiritual and corporeal man, and, by analogy, it is also seen as the very center of God as he opens himself up to man (1 Sam. 13, 14).

In the Old Testament, the heart is still largely understood as the seat of spiritual energy and of thought, while the bosom or "bowels" (as in "bowels of mercy": *rachamim*, *splanchna*) are rather taken to be the seat of the affections. In the New Testament, however, both aspects coincide with the concept of "heart." Having one's "whole heart" turned to God means the opening of the whole man towards him (Acts 8,37; Mt. 22,37). Thus, the heart that was hardened (Mk. 10,5, following numerous parallels in the Old Testament) must be renewed: from a stony heart it must become a heart of flesh (Ez. 11,19, etc.; cf. 2 Cor. 3,3).

In the wake of Homer, Greek philosophy saw in the heart the center of psychic and spiritual life: for Stoicism, the heart is the seat of the *hēgemonikon*, the guiding faculty in man. Going beyond this, New Testament theology adds, on the one hand, an incarnational element. The soul is wholly incarnate in the heart, and, in the heart, the body wholly becomes the medium for the expression of the soul. At the same time, the New Testament adds an element of personhood: it is first in Christianity that the entire man—

body and soul—becomes a unique person through God's call and, with his heart, orients towards God this uniqueness that is his.

The narrative of the piercing with the spear and of the outpouring of blood and water should be read as being continuous with the Johannine symbolism of water, spirit and blood, to which also belong the references to "thirst." Earthly water again makes thirsty, but Jesus' water quenches thirst forever (4,13f.). "Let whoever is thirsty come to me and drink as one believing in me" (7,37f.); thus the believer's thirst is quenched forever (6,35). Related to this is the extraordinary promise that, in him who drinks it, Jesus' water would become a fountain leaping up to life eternal (4,14), which is supported by the verse of Scripture: "Streams of living water will spring from his belly" (*koilia*: 7,38). It is at the moment when Jesus suffers the most absolute thirst that he dissolves, to become an eternal fountain. That verse may refer to the ever-present analogy between water and word/spirit (Jesus' words are "spirit and life"). Even better, it may be related to the "fountain" in Ezechiel's new temple (Ez. 47; cf. Zach. 13,1), with which Jesus compared his own body (2,21).

In the context of John's general symbolism, there can be no doubt that in the outpouring of blood and water the evangelist saw the institution of the sacraments of eucharist and baptism (cf. Cana: 2,1ff.; the unity of water and spirit: 3,5; and of water, spirit and blood: 1 Jn. 5,6, with explicit reference to "Jesus

15

Christ: he it is that has come by water and blood").
The opening of the Heart is the handing over of what
is most intimate and personal for the use of all. All
may enter the open, emptied space. Moreover, official
proof had to be provided that the separation of flesh
and blood had been realized to the full as a prerequis-
ite for the form of the eucharistic meal. Both the
(new) temple and the newly opened fountain where
all may drink point to community. The surrendered
Body is the locus where the new covenant is established, where the new community assembles. It is at
once space, altar, sacrifice, meal, the community and
its spirit.

PART ONE

THE KINGDOM

CHAPTER I

THE FLOWING STREAM

P RISONS OF FINITUDE! Like every other being, man is born in many prisons. Soul, body, thought, intuition, endeavor: everything about him has a limit, is itself tangible limitation; everything is a This and a That, different from other things and shunned by them. From the grilled windows of the senses each person looks out to the alien things which he will never be. Even if his spirit could fly through the spaces of the world like a bird, he himself will never be this space, and the furrow which he traces in the air vanishes immediately and leaves no lasting impression. How far it is from one being to its closest neighbor! And even if they love each other and wave to one another from island to island, even if they attempt to exchange solitudes and pretend they have unity, how much more painfully does disappointment then fall upon them when they touch the invisible bars—the cold glass pane against which they hurl themselves like captive birds. No one can tear down his own dungeon; no one knows who inhabits the next cell. Conjecture can grope its way from man to woman, from child to adult, even less than it can from human being to animal. Beings are alien to one another, even if they do stand beautifully by one another and complement one another like colors, like water and stone, like sun and fog: even if they do communally perfect the resounding harmony of the universe. Variegation pays the price of a bitter separation. The mere fact of existing as an individual constitutes renunciation. The limpid mirror has been shattered, the infinite image has been shattered over the face of the world, the world has become a heap of fragments. But every single splinter remains precious, and from each fragment there flashes a ray of the mystery of its origin. And infinite good can be detected in the finite good: the promise of greater things, the possibility of breaking through, an enticement so sweet that our pulse falters for keen delight, when the marvel—conferring a boundless bliss—suddenly discloses itself for a few moments, free of its concealment, and presents itself open and naked, stripped of the ashen garment of custom. Here is the seal of its provenance, the kiss of its origin, the pledge of its lost unity. Yet the kernel of this delight always remains incomprehensible and mysterious. If one should snatch at it, he will not grasp it; he will hold the apple of Adam in his hand, not the infinite fruit from the Tree of Life. Smiling sadly, the heavenly image will slip away, effacing itself and dissolving into fumes. What appeared to be boundless again exhibits its stark walls, and both the seeker and the sought slide back into their narrow prison. Once again we stand over against everything, a part of a part, and what we have can only be imparted. No tugging, no weeping can burst open the prison.

But look: hovering, oscillating, inconceivably flowing Time is there no less—the invisible barque going from shore to shore, a rustling of wings from being to being. Come aboard Time: already it is setting out. It carries you along, and you know neither how nor where it is taking you. The rigid ground under you is already beginning to tremble and give way. The hard road becomes supple and alive, and it begins to flow with all the beauty of a river's meandering course. The banks constantly change and vary: now it is woods through which Time rocks you, now far-reaching fields and the cities of men. The stream itself has many forms and modulations: now it flows with a gentle rush, now it plunges wildly into cataracts, then it again flows smoothly and widens into a lake. The movement now becomes imperceptible, and along the banks the water at times flows backward until it is again gripped by the pull from the center.

Space is cold and stiff, but Time is alive. Space divides, but Time brings everything to everything else. It does not course outside of you and you do not swim upon it like a drifting log. Time flows through you: you yourself are in flow. You are the river. Are you grieving? Trust Time: soon you will be laughing. Are you laughing? You cannot hold fast your laughter, for soon you will be weeping. You are blown from mood to mood, from one state to another, from waking to sleeping and from sleeping again to waking. You cannot go on wandering for long. You come to a halt, you are tired, you are hungry, you must sit down, you eat, you stand up again, you begin anew to wander. You suffer: from the distance, unattainable, you glimpse the Deed for which you long. But the stream is constantly moving you and one morning the hour of action has arrived. You are a child, and never (so you think) will you escape the helplessness of childhood, which locks you into four windowless walls. But look: your wall is itself movable and yielding, and your whole being becomes refashioned into a youth. From within yourself there rise hidden springs that leap up to yourself. Possibilities open up before you like flowers, and one day the world has grown all around you. Softly, Time transports you from one curve to another. New vistas and horizons unfold at your side as you pass by. You begin to love the change: you've discovered an extraordinary adventure is afoot. You sense a direction, you feel a new impulse, you can smell the sea. And you see that what changes in you changes also in everything around you. Every point you hurriedly pass by is itself in movement. Every point is being whirled in some direction: its own long history is following its course: but each point knows the ending of its history no more than you know that of yours. You glance up to heaven. Sublime is the rotation of its suns, but these are each heavily laden with their planetary systems as with grapes, and they dash away from one another into already-prepared distances and unfathomable spaces. You smash atoms and they swarm about in more confusion than if you had stamped your foot on an anthill. You seek a mainstay and a permanent law in the temperate mid-region of our earth, but here, too, there is nothing but constant event and changing history, and no one can forecast for you even next week's clouds.

A law does indeed exist, but it is the mysterious law of transformation, to be fathomed by none except the person who is himself transformed. You cannot draw the river onto the dry bank, there to trap its imperative to flow, as if it were a fish. And it is only in the water that you yourself can learn how to swim. The wise among men seek to fathom the foundations of existence, but all they can do is to describe one wave of the current. In their portrayal, the flowing has congealed and can again become true only if they repeatedly release the picture they have painted back into change. The greedy among them have launched many projects: they have thrown rocks into the water in order to dam up the stream: in their systems, they contrived to invent an Isle of Eternity, and then they puffed up their hearts like balloons, all of it so as to catch eternity in the trap of one blissful Now. But they caught only air and they burst, or, turned as if by witchery into an Imaginary Idea, they wholly forgot to live, and the stream calmly washed over their corpses. No: the law is in the river and only by running can you seize it. Perfection lies in fullness of journey. For this reason, never think you have arrived. Forget what lies behind you; reach out for what lies before you. Through the very change in which you lose what you have snatched up you will at last be transformed into what you crave for with such longing.

Trust Time. Time is music, and the space out of which it resounds is the future. Measure by measure, the symphony is created in a dimension that invents itself, and which at each moment makes itself available from an unfathomable store of Time. Space is often lacking: the stone is too small for the statue, the town-square cannot contain the multitude. When has Time ever been lacking? When has it run out like too short a piece of string? Time is as long as grace. Entrust yourself to the grace of Time. You cannot interrupt music in order to catch and hoard it. Let it flow and flee, otherwise you cannot grasp it. You cannot condense it into one beautiful chord and thus possess it once and for all. Patience is the first virtue of the one who wants to perceive. And the second is renunciation. For look: you cannot grasp the melody's flight until its last note has sounded. Only now, when the whole melody has died away, can you survey its mysterious balances, the arcs of tension and the curves of distance. Only what has set in the ear can rise in the heart. And therefore (and yet!), you cannot grasp invisibly in the unity of the spirit what you have not sensibly experienced in the manifoldness of the senses. And so the eternal is above time and is its harvest, and yet it comes to be and is realized only through the change of time.

What strange beings we are! We grow only by being thrust into transiency. We cannot ripen, we cannot become rich in any way other than by an uninterrupted renunciation that occurs hour by hour. We must endure duration and outlast it. Whenever we attempt to stop we violate the very life-principle of nature. Whenever we lose the patience of an existence in time, by that very fact we fall into nothingness. As long as we walk on, a voice whispers to us from the contrary wind we are cleaving; but if we halt in silence the better to hear it, already it is muted. Time is at once a threat and an unheard-of promise. "Let me course on," it calls to us, "otherwise you won't be able to come along! Let go of me, show me your empty hands: otherwise I cannot fill them! Otherwise I will pass you by with my fresh new gifts and abandon you to your outdated baubles. Believe me: you are richer if you are able to end and break off your glee and your hour of triumph, richer if you can be poor and open instead, a beggar at the gate of the future! Don't hold on, don't cling or clasp! You cannot hoard time: let it teach you to squander! Squander yourself what another must otherwise take from you with violence. Then you, the robbed miser, will be richer than a king. Time is the school of exuberance, the school of magnanimity."

It is the grand school of love. And if time is the ground of our existence, then the ground of our existence is love. Time is existence flowing on: love is life that pours itself forth. Time is existence that has been dispossessed, defenseless and unasked; love dispossesses itself and willingly allows itself to be disarmed. Existence cannot help it (this its law and its essence): by its flowing it demonstrates love. And so the way is open for existence to be itself love. We must be patient even if we are perishing from impatience, for no one can increase the span of his life by even the smallest increment, except, that is, by growing . . . with time. We must renounce things even if, shaking with greed, we clutch our possessions: quietly does deadly Time remove our fingers, and the treasures we've snatched tumble to the ground. Every moment in our life teaches us with gentleness what the last moment must finally enforce with violence: that we ought to discover in the mystery of time's duration the sweet core of our life—the offer made by a tireless love. Strange: we *may* be what we vainly long after. We can realize simply in our existence what we so painfully fail to achieve in our knowing and willing. We would like to give ourselves away, and we have already been given away. We look for one to whom we could abandon ourselves, and already we have long been accepted. And when the heart becomes knotted when it considers the uselessness of all it has lived through, this is but the fear of the bride on her wedding-night when she is robbed of her last veil.

We have been designed as beings who may willingly accomplish what they must unwillingly desire. But what can bring more bliss, what thought can be more intoxicating than this: already to exist is a work of love! And so, it is in vain that I fight being what I have always been . . . And even if I should cry out "No!" at the top of my voice, even if my veins should swell with fear as I shout this "No!", even then, in the last corner of the cave, an echo would treacherously say yes: Yes! If, after many a death, we die for one last time, in this act of highest life existence has ceased dying. Only one thing can ever be deadly: to be alive and not to want to die. Every death which is willingly died is a source of life. The cup of love is thus a mixture of life and death. It is a miracle that we do not love: love is the watermark in the parchment of our existence. It is to love's melody that our limbs respond. Whoever loves is obeying the impulse of life in time; whoever refuses to love is struggling (uselessly) against the current. How easy the gesture of giving becomes for us when the golden water of Being constantly runs through us as through the mouth of a wellspring! How easy to become dispossessed when we are bathing in the wealth of a future that flows on inexhaustibly! How easy is fidelity when faithless Time has placed its inviolable ring on our finger! How easy is death when we experience hourly how blessed, indeed, how advantageous it is to pass on! And even aging, anxious aging, which contracts and reduces us, offers as a substitute for exterior mists the inner clarity of poverty. There is nothing tragic about us, for every renunciation is extravagantly rewarded, and the more we approach the pure center of naked poverty, the more intimately do we take possession of ourselves, the more reliably are all things our own.

Thus, we may be what we would like to be. In the mysterious water of Time in which we bathe and which is ourselves, in this liquid of Being, the heart's deeply hated resistance is dissolved and outdone. Only what is fixed is questionable, only what is opaque and stiff and puts up a resistance to every spirit and eye. But the eye is moist and the spirit translucent, and so its rays pierce through and dissolve what is stubborn. While we outwardly armor ourselves with layer upon layer against life's inexorable imperatives, in our inmost being the spring leaps forth and washes away the walls and undermines our most solid fortification. No one can withstand to the end the relentless battering by these billows. Day after day they erode us, gnawing away pebble by pebble at our wasted banks. In the end we collapse. With time even the greatest fool grasps Time. Time hollows out its bed in him and grinds him down with its round stone as the waterfall does a glacier.

Thus it is that you sense Time, and it initiates you into its highest mystery. You come to feel Time's rhythm, now rushing on, now withdrawing. Under the form of the future it approaches you, overwhelms you, bestows on you an immeasurable bounty; but it also robs you and demands that you give everything. It wants you to be at once rich and poor, ever richer and ever poorer. It wants you to be more loving. And if you were once to follow wholeheartedly the law and imperative of your very being, if you were once fully yourself, you would live solely on this gift that flows out to you (this gift which you yourself are), and you would do this by giving it away in turn, in holiness without having defiled it through possessiveness. Your life would be like breath itself, like the lungs' calm and unconscious double movement. And you yourself would be the air, drawn in and exhaled with the changing measure of the tides. You would be the blood in the pulse of a Heart that takes you in and expels you and keeps you captive in the circulation and spell of its veins.

You sense Time and yet have not sensed this Heart? You feel the stream of grace which rushes into you, warm and red, and yet have not felt how you are loved? You seek for a proof, and yet you yourself are that proof. You seek to entrap him, the Unknown One, in the mesh of your knowledge, and yet you yourself are entrapped in the inescapable net of his might. You would like to grasp, but you yourself are already grasped. You would like to overpower and are yourself being overpowered. You pretend to be seeking, but you have long (and for all time) been found. Through a thousand garments you feel your way to a living body, and yet you insist you cannot feel the hand that nakedly touches your bare soul? You jerk about in the haste of your unquiet heart and call it religion, when in truth these are the convulsions of a fish struggling on shipboard. You would like to find God even though it be with a thousand sorrows: what humiliation that your efforts were but an empty fuss, since he has long held you in his hand. Put your finger to the living pulse of Being. Feel the throbbing that in one single act of creation at once claims you and leaves you free. Feel the throbbing that, in the tremendous outpouring of existence, at the same time determines the precise measure of distance: how you ought to love him as your most intimate friend and how you ought to fall down before him as the all-high Lord; how in one and the same act he clothes you out of love and strips you out of love; how, along with existence, he presses all treasures into your hand, and the most precious jewel of all: to love him in return, to be able to give him a gift in return; and how he nevertheless (not afterwards, in a second movement, in a further step) again takes away everything he has given so that you love not the gift but the giver and so that you know, even in giving, that you are but a wave in his stream. In the same split instant of existence you are near and far; in the same moment a friend and a master is set before you. In the same moment you are child and slave. You will never go beyond this first state of things. In eternity you will live as that which you have been. For, even if your virtue, your wisdom, your love towered immeasurably, even if you were to grow beyond men and angels straight through to the highest heaven: even then you would never leave your point of departure. Yet nothing is more blessed than this first moment, and would that on the longest arc of development you would but constantly be curving back to this marvel of your origin! For love's full reality is inconceivably glorious.

And life, to be sure, strives away from its origin. It seeks itself and believes that it finds itself where it is safe from the dangers of its beginnings. The seed seems to be all too unprotected; it seems to need a strong bark, and the moment of generation appears all too close to nothingness. But an iron law compels all linear motion back into the circle. Life awakens to its own reality and rises up in a great, slender arch; it then seeks to assert itself on this narrow ridge. Blood flows mightily through the narrow door of an individual's life, making his heart and brain swell. Possessed by a sense of self-importance and of mission, his hands proudly dispense, as if they had created it, what has in fact come to him from afar, from the unknown roots of his forebears. But the summit of the pass has been reached, and while for others the sun may still be climbing, his path begins to descend and plunges into the afternoon of cooler woods, and again he hears it murmuring—a small brook at first: the memory of younger days, now almost buried, begins to swell up in him; a longing for primal times softly comes to life; a presentiment swells up; love is in the ascendancy; and unawares, precipitously, a waterfall suddenly plunges into the abysmal night of the Beginning. All of that marvelous separate existence dissolves, like the course of different rivers, in the One Ocean of death and life. In the One Ocean the waves rise and sink; body floats past body; figures and generations, century after century, are all so much foam falling prostrate on the broad beach of eternity in a most tremendous obeisance.

The meaning of our life: to show our recognition that we are not God. Thus, we die unto God, for God is eternal life. How could we attain to it other than through death? In our life, death is the pledge that we are touching on something that outlives this life. Death is our life's profound bow, the ceremony of *proskynesis* before the Creator's throne. And, since the creatures' innermost being consists of the praise and service and awe which they owe their Creator, a drop of death is commingled in every moment of existence. Because time and love are so closely intertwined, however, creatures also love their dying, and their being does not refuse to perish. But even if the small, individual life should be fearful and our darkened self-will should struggle against death, existence itself—the deep sea-swell that raises and lowers it—knows its Master and gladly bows down before him. For it knows intuitively that autumn comes only to prepare for the spring, and that in this world there willingly wilts whatever bears the promise of blossoming in God.

Thus does the creature die unto God and rise up unto God. We rush into the light and are drawn on in ecstasy; but the fire which no one may approach holds us in its spell. We plunge into the flames, are burnt through and through, but the flame does not kill: it transforms us into light and burns on in us as love. This is love that knows the depths. It lives in us, establishes itself within us as a center; we live from it; it fills and nourishes us; it draws us into its spell, clothing itself with us as with a mantle and using our soul as its organ. This is no longer ourselves: in a most immediate, hardly distinguishable proximity, this is the Lord in us. A loving fear grows within us, fear which again and more urgently forces us to our knees, into the dust of nothingness. Mightily, more roaring than Time itself, the Heart of love hammers on. It pulses and unites Two into One, or again divides One into Two. Thus do we live from God: he draws us mightily into his glowing core and robs us with his lordliness of every center that is not his own. But we are not God, and, in order the more mightily to show us the power of his center, he hurls us out imperiously—not alone, not powerless, but endowed with our own center and in the power of his mission. God claims us jealously; he wants us solely for himself and for his honor. But, laden with his love and living from his honor, he sends us back into the world. For it is not the rhythm of his creation that it should go out from God as by egress and return to its source as by regress. Rather are both these things as one, inseparable, and the going forth is no less unconditional than the return, nor the mission less God-willed than the longing for God. And perhaps the going forth from God is still more divine than the return home to God, since the greatest thing is not for us to know God and reflect this knowledge back to him as if we were gleaming mirrors, but for us to proclaim God as burning torches proclaim the light. "I am the light of the world," says God, "and without me you can do nothing. And, beside me, there is no light and no god. But you are the light of the world, a borrowed but not a false light; burning with my flame you are to enkindle the world with my fire. Go out into the furthest darkness! Take my love like lambs into the midst of wolves! Take my gospel to those who cower in the dark and in the shadow of death! Go out; venture beyond the well-guarded fold! I once brought you home when you were lost lambs and were bleeding among the thorns. Then did I bring you home on my good shepherd's shoulders. But now the flock is scattered and the gate of the pen gapes wide: this is the hour of mission! Out! Separate yourselves from me, for I am with you until the end of the world. For I myself went out from the Father and, by going out from him, I became obedient unto death, and by obeying I became the perfect image of his love for me. The going out itself is love; the going out itself is the return. Just as the Father has sent me, so do I send you. Going out from me as a ray from the sun, as a stream from its source, you remain in me, for I myself am the ray that flashes forth, the stream that is poured out from the Father. To give is more blessed than to receive. Just as I radiate the Father, so also are you to radiate me. So turn your face to me that I can turn it out into the world. You are to be so separated from your own ways that I can place you on the way that I am.

This is a new mystery, inconceivable to mere creatures: that even distance from God and the coolness of reverence are an image and a likeness of God and of divine life. What is most incomprehensible is, in fact, the truest reality: precisely by not being God do you resemble God. And precisely by being outside of God are you in God. For to be over against God is itself a divine thing. As a person who is incomparable you reflect the uniqueness of your God. For in God's unity, too, there are found distance and reflection and eternal mission: Father and Son over against one another and yet one in the Spirit and in the nature that seals the Three of them together. Not only the Primal Image is God, but also the Likeness and the Reflected Image. Not only the unity is unconditional; it is also divine to be Two when there is a Third that binds them together. For this reason was the world created in this Second One, and in this Third One does it abide in God.

But the meaning of creation remains unexplainable so long as the veil covers the eternal Image. This life would be nothing but destiny, this time only sorrow, all love but decay, if the pulse of Being did not throb in the eternal, triune Life. Only then does the spring of life begin to leap up also in us: it speaks in us of the Word, becomes itself Word and Language, and communicates to us—as a greeting from God—the task of proclaiming the Father in the world. Only then is the curse of solitude also resolved: for, to-be-over-against is itself divine, and all beings—man and woman and animal and stone—are not, by their particular existence, excluded from the common life, rather are they oriented to one another in their very form. They are not locked up in a dark dungeon from which their oppressed yearning seeks to escape out into the unbounded: rather, as God's messengers accomplishing a resplendent work of completion, they are rounded out into the one Body whose Head rests in the bosom of the Father.

Beat on, then, Heart of existence, pulse of Time! Instrument of eternal love! You make us rich and, then again, you make us poor. You draw us to yourself only then yourself to withdraw from us. But, through the surges of the tide, we remain the festal ornament you wear. Majestically you roar on over us; you reduce us to silence with your stars; you fill us to overflowing, to the very brim, and you empty us down to the dregs, to the point of collapse. And whether you roar or keep silence, whether you fill up or empty out, you remain the Lord and we your household servants.

CHAPTER II

THE COMING OF THE LIGHT

H E CAME INTO THE WORLD, laden with the wisdom and knowledge of the Father, endowed with all the treasures of the abyss—he, the Expression of the Ineffable. In the beginning he is the Word. And when he opened his mouth before the world and began to speak of the Father, then he began to express himself also, for he is the living Word, at once Speaker and Speech. He came into the world in order to reveal himself as the revelation of the Father. By concentrating into this proclamation all of his endeavor and the meaning of his very being, by wanting to be nothing other than the mirror and window of the Father, the will and essence of them both coincided precisely, and this unity was the Holy Spirit. Thus, threefold was the Deed and threefold the Content of revelation, as also the essence and kernel of whatever truth was encompassed by the Trinity—root and goal of all things.

In this Speech, the Word of God was love. For that person loves who opens himself up in order to communicate himself, and this is what God did with his Word. The act of speaking was itself God's love, and therefore also the utterance. In other words, the speaking was itself nothing other than the utterance, for the Word was with God and God was the Word. A source began to flow, and the source consisted precisely in having begun to flow. There were enough dead cisterns in the world, but the newness of the thing was that a water was running and flowing from itself. God's cup had flowed over with plenty; from wrath, one could have thought. But when God thunders, the cloud of wrath pours out a rustling of love.

Down hurtles the water, and love, too, draws it (this its gravity) down to the earth. What comes from above has no need of heights. It needs the depths; it longs to experience the abyss. What comes from above is already pure and protected; it can reveal itself only by a descent. What comes from below naturally strives for the heights. Its impulse presses on to the light; its impetus a seeking of power. Every finite spirit wants to assert itself and luxuriantly unfurl its leafy crown in the sun of existence. Whatever is poor wants to be rich—rich in power, in warmth, through wisdom and sympathy. This is the law of the world. For all things strive to pass from enveloped seed to fully developed life. The possible impatiently presses on towards form. The obscure must move towards the light through rubble and earth. And in this general onrush, creatures collide and place limits on each other, and these limits are movable in the play and strife over existence, and the borders between creatures are called custom, convention, family and state.

In its own way, this onrush, this entelechy, witnesses to the Creator's essential goodness, since everything that is good rushes on to develop beyond itself. It witnesses to the creature's dark drive towards God, for this impulse is restless and full of hunger, and to appease its emptiness insatiably swallows up into itself world, men and God. This is why, from all antiquity, the love of man has been termed poor and needy, in need of the beautiful to beget, drunk and blind, something worthy of love.

The Word, however, came from above. It came from the fullness of the Father. In the Word there was no urge since it was itself the fullness. In him was light and life and love without lust, love which had compassion for the void, willing to fill up what was hollow. But it was the essence of the void itself to press on to fullness. It was a menacing void, a chasm fitted with teeth. The light came into the darkness, but the darkness had no eye for the light: it had only jaws. The light came to illumine those who sit in the shadow of tombs, and such illumination required that the radiance of the light be recognized and that one be oneself transformed into streaming light. This would mean the death of the urge and its resurrection as love.

Man wants to soar up, but the Word wants to descend. Thus will the two meet half-way, in the middle, in the place of the Mediator. But they will cross like swords cross; their wills are opposed to one another. For God and man are related in a manner far different from man and woman: in no way do they complete one another. And we may not say that, to show his fullness, God needs the void, as man needs fullness to nourish his void. Nor that God descends so that man may ascend. If this were the mediation, then man would indeed have swallowed God's love up into himself, but only as fodder and fuel for his addictive urge. His will to power would finally have overpowered God, and thus the Word would be strangled and the darkness would not have grasped it. And man's final condition would be worse than his first, for he would have encircled in the narrow spell of his ego not only his fellow-man, but also the Creator himself, degrading him to the role of a lever for his egotistic yearning.

But if, rather, they were really to encounter one another, what road had to be followed? The darkness had to become brighter; blind urge had to pass over into a love that sees; and the clever will to possess and develop had to be transfigured into the foolish wisdom that pours itself out. And then a new instruction was issued: instead of going past God's Word in its descent and pursuing the rash ascent to the Father, we are now to turn around and, along with the Word, go back down the steps we have climbed, find God on the road *to* the world, on no road other than that by which the Son journeys on towards the Father. For only love redeems. Yet, what love is God only knows, for God is love. There are not two sorts of love. There is not, alongside God's love, another, human love. Rather, when God so determines and he proclaims his Word, love then descends, love then flows out into the void, and God has set up his claim and his emblem over every love.

But how is man ever to grasp this? For the impulse and drive and yearning of his nature have long since hardened into sin, and the illness of the will-to-ego has eaten away the tissues of his soul like a cancer. The rich heart which God bestows on man flared full of desires and consumed itself with melancholy. Every attempt to break out of his interior prison only cast man into a more ruthless servitude. Grown pliant to coercion, he began to glorify the hard labor he had despised, erecting a rampart and digging a trench around the tyrannical castle of his ego. Whoever would declare war against this ego had better beware! He would have to fight bout after bout. Even if the enemy were already storming the bridge, even if the castle were already in flames, even if only one tower still put up desperate resistance—even then man would not surrender until the last door had been rammed, the last arrow shot, the last ounce of strength drained from his arms by wrestling to the death.

The Word, then, came into the world—came to what was his, but those who were his did not receive him. He beamed into the gloom, but the darkness turned away. Thus had love's revelation to choose a struggle of life and death. God came into the world, but a bristling barrier of spears and shields was his welcome. His grace began to trickle, but the world made itself supple and impenetrable, and the drops fell to the ground. The world was hermetically closed. Closed the cycle of human life, ascending from the womb and bent on returning to the womb. Closed, too, the society of men, self-sufficient and self-satisfied. All man's yearning beyond his confines was incessantly deflected back into those confines. Closed his religion, and reduced to a circle of observances and rites, prayer-formulas and sacrifices, the efforts of men and the deity's return in kind, all of it coming down from the ancestors and to be tampered with by none but the impious. Closed and well-armored was the world against God from all sides, and it had no eyes to look out since all of its glances were turned inwards on itself. But its interior resembled a hall of mirrors in which the finite appeared refracted as far as the eye could see, multiplying itself infinitely and thus playing the self-sufficient god. Only the world's gullet gaped outwards, ready to swallow down whoever dared approach.

And now that God's Word saw that his descent could entail nothing but his own death and ruination—that his light must sink down into the gloom—he accepted the battle and the declaration of war. And he devised the unfathomable ruse: he would plunge, like Jonas, into the monster's belly and thus penetrate to death's innermost lair; he would experience the farthest dungeon of sin's mania and drink the cup down to the dregs; he would offer his brow to man's incalculable craze for power and violence; in his

42

own futile mission, he would demonstrate the futility of the world; in his impotent obedience to the Father, he would visibly show the impotence of revolt; through his own weakness unto death he would bring to light the deathly weakness of such a despairing resistance to God; he would let the world do its will and thereby accomplish the will of the Father; he would grant the world its will, thereby breaking the world's will; he would allow his own vessel to be shattered, thereby pouring himself out; by pouring out one single drop of the divine Heart's blood he would sweeten the immense and bitter ocean. This was intended to be the most incomprehensible of exchanges: from the most extreme opposition would come the highest union, and the might of his supreme victory was to prove itself in his utter disgrace and defeat. For his weakness would already be the victory of his love for the Father, reconciliation in the eyes of the Father, and, as a deed of his supreme strength, this weakness would be so great that it would far surpass and sustain in itself the world's pitiful feebleness. He alone would henceforth be the measure and thus also the meaning of all impotence. He wanted to sink so low that in the future all falling would be a falling into him, and every streamlet of bitterness and despair would henceforth run down into his lowermost abyss.

No fighter is more divine than one who can achieve victory through defeat. In the instant when he receives the deadly wound, his opponent falls to the

43

ground, himself struck a final blow. For he strikes love and is thus himself struck by love. And by letting itself be struck, love proves what had to be proven: that it is indeed love. Once struck, the hate-filled opponent recognizes his boundaries and understands: behave as he pleases, nevertheless he is bounded on every side by a love that is greater than he. Everything he may fling at love—insults, indifference, contempt, scornful derision, murderous silence, demonic slander—all of it can ever but prove love's superiority; and the blacker the night, the more radiant does love emerge from it. For all worldly life must, if not repeatedly, then at least once bow down before death; life must tread across death's threshold bent over with impotence. In this passageway, life at last repeats the gesture of the Son who confers meaning and shape on every form of impotence. All around we are enclosed by a ubiquitous and deadly boundary, and we—who still believed we could either exclude God from our enclosed space or shut him up in it—we, I say, have through our efforts proved the exclusiveness of his love, which holds us tight in its inescapable arms. For death—our death—has already become one of love's garments and transformations.

But God's plan and ruse are not yet perfected; the most central feat is still lacking. The means is still lacking by which to penetrate into the world's interior in order to transform it from within—the talisman with which to break open the bolted gate. Then it was that God created a Heart for himself and placed it at the center of the world. It was a human Heart, and

44

it knew the impulses and yearnings of human hearts, was experienced in all the windings and wanderings, changes of weather and drives—in a word, experienced in all the bitter joy and joyful bitterness which any human heart has ever savored. The human heart: most foolish, most obstinate, most fickle of all creatures; the seat of all fidelity and of all treachery; an instrument richer than a full orchestra and poorer than a grasshopper's empty chirping; in its incomprehensibility a mirror image of God's own incomprehensibility. This it was that he drew from the world's rib as it slept, and he fashioned it into the organ of his divine love. With this weapon he already stood in the middle of enemy territory, like the warrior in the belly of the Trojan horse, and he already shared fully in the world's bustle, knew all from within.

As in a dream, he could listen in this conch to mankind's sea of blood. Man's betrayal was already betrayed to him, and, like Hagen, he recognized the unprotected spot on Siegfried's invulnerable, horn-covered neck.[1] For in the heart's interior all mystery lies open and displayed, and the waves of the blood carry it, defenseless and wholly unmasked, from one man's heart to another's. It was in this circulation that he shared.

Henceforth his death could not be prevented. For what heart can protect itself? It would not at all be a

[1]See *Niebelungenlied*, III (57), XV (26–28) and XVI (65/66). Trans. Note.

heart if it were armored and jacketed. It would not at all be a heart if it did not gape wide and make itself defenseless to the stream rushing in, if it did not dispense life from its own inexhaustible store of life, forgetting all else for the sheer glee of such lavish squandering. Every heart is drunk with so much blood that its sole occupation it is to make sluggishness leap up into a new dance. A wild zeal consumes the heart; inexorably it beats love's rhythm and the echo of its tyrannical whip rumbles on, even in sleep, and through to the body's most distant members. Heart and life, heart and source, heart and birth are all one: for when had a heart ever time to think of struggle and resistance? While the limbs are all aslumber and succumb to the temptation of death, it is the sleepless heart which keeps the unconscious sleepers alive. These have the chance to defend themselves: they are expected to overcome the enemy without, and it is the unarmed heart which gives them the needed strength from the fiery center. All war is nourished from the heart, and yet it itself is peace. All power comes from the heart, and yet it itself is impotence. All health flows out from this incessantly bubbling wound.

Every heart is unprotected because it is the source. This is why every enemy aims at the heart. Here is the abode of life, and here is where life may be struck down. Here is where life climbs out of the gorge of nothingness naked with the freshness of youth. Here is where you may place your finger on the artery of existence and with your eyes see its miraculous birth. Red on red, the Rose of Life breaks open and the eye plunges into it and into the mystery of primal generation. All else radiates from this creative center. When the veins return here after their long wandering, what had flowed out flows back tired and dark to immerse itself anew in the pulsation of its origin, and the limp warmth that is brought back is still an echo of the beginning. Every mystery of life has its origin in the heart. Heavily laden with mystery, life's fleets sail from the harbor on waves of blood. And what they bring home from far-off islands, what they whisper into the great maternal ear of the beginning: could it be something new, more alive than life itself? Life utters itself in the heart's undying hammer-strokes, and the heart's expansions and contractions, its openings and closings, the to-and-fro of its blood all extend to become the very life-principle of the whole body.

And so, the Word came into the world. Eternal Life selected for itself the abode of a human Heart. And it resolved to live within this trembling tent; it deigned to let itself be struck. His death was thus a settled affair. For the source of life is defenseless. Within his eternal citadel, in his inaccessible light, God had been unassailable. The arrows of sin ricocheted from his brazen majesty as if they were children's play-darts. But God housed in a heart! How easy he now was to reach! How swiftly he could be hurt! More easily than a man, for a man is not only a heart, but bones and cartilage, tough muscle-fiber and hardened skin: one

47

must really have a grim intention to wound a man. But what a target a heart is! what an enticement! The gun points almost unconsciously in that direction. How exposed God had made himself! What folly he committed! He had himself betrayed the weak spot of his love. No sooner will the news become known that he is dwelling among us as a Heart than each and every one will begin to whet his arrows and test his bow. A shower, a hailstorm will fall upon him, millions of shots fly towards the tiny red spot.

Nor will his unprotected Heart protect him. For a heart has no understanding: it does not know why it is beating. His Heart will not stand by him. It will (every heart is faithless) betray him. For, indeed, it never stands still: it always goes on, it runs. And because love always runs over, his Heart will also run over—over to the enemy as a deserter. It is his pleasure to abide among the children of men; it is his curiosity to know the taste of other, alien hearts. He wanted to savor this taste, and though it must be for a price, this price he willingly paid. Unto all eternity he will not forget this taste. Only a heart could be commissioned with such adventures, follies best left concealed from reason, best left unspoken. Such can only be devised in a conspiracy with flesh and blood: follies of the poor heart which knows how to conjure up treasures out of its hidden poverty and the scanty estate of an earthly acre—treasures before which the dwellers of heaven stand in amazement.

Thus did the Son come into the world, and his Heart dragged him only God knows where, for every heart impatiently tugs at the leash. It scents tracks which no one else knows are there. It slips off on its own ways. And yet, in the end, they are in accord, the Lord and his Heart. The Heart willingly follows the will of the Lord, who incites it to rush into the fox's lair. And the Lord follows willingly the tracks of his Heart, which makes him stray off to deadly adventures: the hunt for men in the virgin-forest of a dark world hostile to God.

Incomprehensible sign, set up in the world's midst, between heaven and earth! Composite body, like that of a centaur, in which were alloyed what ought to remain eternally separated by the distance of awe! The divine Ocean forced into the tiny wellspring of a human Heart! The mighty oak-tree of divinity planted in the small, fragile pot of an earthly Heart! God, sublime on the throne of his majesty, and the Servant—toiling with sweat and kneeling in the dust of adoration—no longer to be distinguished from one another! The eternal God's awareness of his kingship pressed into the nescience of human abasement! All the treasures of God's wisdom and knowledge stored in the narrow chamber of human poverty! The vision of the eternal Father shrouded in the intuitions of faith's obscurity! The rock of divine certainty floating on the tides of an earthly hope! The triangle of the Trinity balanced by one tip upon a human Heart!

Thus does this Heart hover between heaven and earth like the narrow passage in an hourglass, and incessantly the sand of grace trickles from the upper compartment down to the earthly bottom. Then again, through that tight duct, a weak aroma rises from below to penetrate the upper spheres, a scent foreign to the heavens, and no portion of the infinite Godhead remains untouched by this new perfume. Softly and steadily a reddish vapor begins to tint the white regions of the angels, and the unapproachable love of Father and Son acquires the color of tenderness and of heartfelt affection. All of God's mysteries, which until now had hidden their countenance under six wings, disclose themselves and smile down at men. For in the mirror of the earthly region God's mysteries unexpectedly see their own countenance reflected, as if they now had a double.

Everything that had been one becomes double, and everything double becomes one. It is not a pale image of heavenly truth that is acted out on earth; it is the heavenly reality itself, translated into earthly language. When the Servant here below falls to the ground tired and spent from the burden of his day's labor, when his head touches the earth to adore his God, this poor gesture captures in itself all of the uncreated Son's homage before his Father's throne. And the gesture forever adds to this eternal perfection the laborious, painful, inconspicuous, lusterless perfection of a human being's humility. But never had the Father loved the Son with such ultimacy as when he beheld him collapse to his knees in exhaustion. At that moment he swore to himself that he would raise this Child over all the heavens, even to his paternal Heart—this Son of Man who was also his Son—and that, for the sake of this One, he would raise up also all of the others who resembled him, his greatly Beloved—all of those in whom he could discern the traits of his Son, even in their distortion and concealment. And when the Servant, as his hangmen's plaything, covered over with blood and crowned with' thorns, so greatly conceals his countenance that even he, the Father, finds the murderer to be more human and acquits him, while the mob, bellowing, hunts down to his death that other One who is no longer his Son: then it is that the divine majesty possessed a glory and splendor never before so perfect, for in that outcast's unrecognizable face there is reflected, spotless and radiant, the will of the Father.

Who can here separate what may no longer be separated? Who can divide God's majesty from man's figure as slave? Who can distinguish, in this God's earthly deeds, what derives from the human instrument from which the ultimate has been drawn and what is a matter of grace, which can elicit from the violin sounds never before heard? Who can determine what a human heart is capable of when, raised above itself, it becomes an expression of the divine and precisely as such is able both to manifest its greatest humanity and to surrender it? Who can point to the borderline between the humanity which an earthly heart contains in itself and that other humanity to which heavenly love can make it expand? And who can say that in that second, heavenly infinity the human heart would have to cease beating, since it would run out of breath, since it could not be expanded to the very limits of the world, indeed, of God himself? Or who can say that a divine person does not have enough room to dwell in a heart thus broadened and that, therefore, the world itself cannot easily and wholly without force find a place in that Heart in the most natural way? Who is presumptuous enough to assert that the finite is enough for us, that a secret happiness in some earthly nook—a few years, a subdued happiness, a modest happiness—is enough for the heart? Who can presume to say that humanity is purer if it is sharply sundered from the divine, if it tastes its own transitoriness and bends down over itself to drink in its own tears as a glorious wine? Who could do this instead of looking up to the great Heart in the center, instead of praising the destruction and defeat of all bonds, giving praise because the Lord of highest heaven has looked upon his creation's lowliness with such love, praising him for having drawn it to himself and for having chosen flesh and blood to be the home and abode of a more than human grace?

Praise, O my heart, the reaches of the Heart of the World! Although the triune ocean of eternal life may thunder from above into our little bowl, so too does the counter-ocean of all lands and times—the crashing tide of the gloomy world, the black sprayfoam of sin—billow up from below to meet it. Everything—treachery and cowardice, spite, fear and disgrace—surges up, presses and crowds into the Heart of the World. And the two oceans crash into one another in that Heart, like fire and water, and the eternal struggle between heaven and hell is decided within that narrow battlefield. Already it should have burst a thousand times under such assault; but it holds fast, perseveres, and triumphs through the ordeal. In one stroke it drains the whole goblet of heaven and hell, and along with the most abject misery it savors the sublimest bliss. And what here exults and weeps ceases not for a single moment to be what it was: a plain human heart. This little Heart will not burst as it holds its ground against the double assault, the double storm of love and hate, the double lightningbolt of judgment and of grace. It will not burst even when the Father, hiding himself, joins the company of his betrayers and forsakes him: alone in the midst of the world, tossed about by the most icy darkness, ablaze with the flames of hell, grinned at by sin's every grimace, filled with unimaginable anguish, buried alive, swallowed up by a bottomless abyss. But even death cannot kill him, and all of hell's waters cannot drown him. And so this Heart (which continues to love even when the Father shuts himself off from him) manifests itself as the greatest of things. Greater still than God's miracles would be the miracles of the human heart. But what we have here is God's human Heart.

For let us not forget: if human limits became capable of receiving God's fullness, this was through a gift of God and not through the creature's own ability to contain it. Only God can expand the finite to infinity without shattering it. And greater still than the miracle that a heart can be extended to God's proportions is the marvel that God was able to shrink to man's proportions; that the Ruler's mind was contained in the mind of the Servant; that the Father's eternal vision, without annulling itself, became blinded even to the blindness of a trampled worm; that the perfect Yes to the Father's will could be uttered in the midst of a storm of impulses impelling the death-tormented Lamb to take flight; that the eternal distance of love between Father and Son (eternally enclosing itself by the embrace of both in the Spirit) could gape wide as the distance between heaven and hell, from whose pit the Son groans his "I thirst," the Spirit now no longer anything but the huge, separating and impassable chaos; that the Trinity could, in suffering's distorted image, so disfigure itself into the relationship between judge and sinner; that eternal love could don the mask of divine wrath; that the Abyss of Being could so deplete itself into an abyss of nothingness.

But even this mystery is taken up and contained within the space of a Heart. In its center Being and Non-Being encounter each other. It alone knows the secret of both the knotting and the untying of the riddle. In its axis the beams cross. Every abyss is bridged by the impetus of his love. Every contradiction grows silent before his word of surrender. Such an undivided Heart is just as much God's love become human as it is man's love become divine. It is the perfect demonstration of the triune life of God and the perfect living out before God of a single-minded conviction. Distance and proximity coincide. The servant is a friend because he is a servant, and the friend is a servant because he is a friend. And nothing is confused or abolished, nor is any boundary violated by the vertigo of such infinities. Precise and clear and solid as crystal do the form and the contour remain, and what sin had scrambled together chaotically now becomes separated by the purity of obedience and reverence. Sober is the intoxication of this love, virginal the bridal bed of heaven and earth.

For it is not ecstasy that redeems, but rather obedience. And it is not freedom that enlarges, but rather our bonds. And so it was that God's Word came into the world bound by the compulsion of love. As the Father's Servant and as the true Atlas, he took the world upon his shoulders. Through his own deeds he joined together the two hostile wills, and, by binding them, he undid the inextricable knot. He dared to exact everything from his Heart; indeed, by over-exacting he wrenched his Heart up to wholly impossible tasks. It was through such overburdening that the Heart recognized its divine Lord, recognized happiness and love (which are always over-exacting), and opened itself up to obedience.

Opened itself up to the world. Took the world up into itself. Became the Heart of the World. Dispossessed itself to become this Heart. The hushed chamber became a military highway on which the caravans of grace descend and the long trains of weepers and beggars go up. Now it is one big hub-bub, a hustle and bustle as at big ports of reshipment or at trade-centers. Everything going up receives here its papers and authorizations: one single Heart handles the quota of a hundred-thousand officials. Everything coming down is here sorted out and distributed. No one may be passed over. Everyone needs assistance and consolation, needs his mission, the precise description of the route ahead of him, his provisions for the road. Huge numbers of petitioners swarm all about, and each case must be handled individually. No one destiny resembles another, and no grace is impersonal. The threads are running; the loom of the world is spinning out its infinite pattern; the sap circulates in mankind's veins; but an enormous fly-wheel brings all of it into motion, an invisible pulse-beat propels it all. The circulation of love begins. God's shovels dig into the depths, haul the dripping mire up from the underworld of souls, and load it onto the Heart at the center. The poisoned blood is drawn in, filtered, and shot out rejuvenated and rosy. All that is toilsome and oppressive is dipped into the loosening bath of mercy. Exhaustion and despair are washed away into the Heart that absorbs them.

This Heart lives on service. It does not seek to glorify itself, but the Father alone. It does not speak of its love. It performs its service so unobtrusively that it is almost forgotten, as we forget our heart under the stress of our affairs. We think that life lives of itself. No one listens to his own heart, not even for a second—his heart, that bestows hour after hour on him. We have grown used to the slight tremor in our being, to the eternal beating of the waves that from within us dash on the shore of consciousness. We accept it as we do our destiny, or nature, or the course of things. We have grown used to love. And we no longer hear the tapping finger that knocks day and night at the gate of our soul; we no longer hear this question, this request to enter.

CHAPTER III

THE BROKEN SUN

T HUS BEGAN HIS DESCENT INTO THE WORLD. "Go there and set it in order," the Father had said. And so he did come, and now he mingled as a stranger in the tumult of the market-place. He walked past the stands where the clever and the witty offered their wares for sale. He saw the vendors' feverish hands as they rummaged through carpets and trinkets. He listened as skilled charlatans praised their own latest inventions: models for state and society, sure guides to the blessed life, machines to fly to the absolute, trapdoors and escapes into a blissful nothingness. He walked past the statues of the gods, the known and the unknown, glanced into the spirit's store-rooms, where bundles and casks were piled high (for man carries in his blood the animal instinct for security and protection), and peered through the curtains of inns where the absinthe of secret knowledge provides admission into artificial paradises and infernos. He climbed a mountain, looked out over the different countries, heard laughing and crying, saw in many a chamber man and woman hotly intertwining, and in the next room a woman in labor, groaning. Dead men were being carried out, past children on their way to school. Cities were being built over the rubble of vanished settlements. Here a war seethed; there peace firmly carried the day. Love laughed out of hatred, and hatred out of a cruel love. The blossoms and the mould, innocence and vice grew hopelessly intertwined, mingled their scents inextricably. A frightful noise, thick with the confusion of a thousand voices, went up from the throng. Dust and smoke whirled about, and everything gave off the sweetish smell of refuse and decay. No one knew the Father's name.

He was the Light, and all were blind. He was the Word, and all were deaf. He was Love, but no one even suspected Love existed. And even when he walked through the crowd and it almost crushed him, no one saw him. He fixed his divine eye on this youth or on that girl, but they did not feel it and looked away in their distraction. In the glittering of the world's night his flame shone more pitifully than a candle in the wind. His voice died away like that of a small bird in the roar of a waterfall. Two worlds crossed in his soul, and it was unbearable to embrace their opposition within one single vision. This everyday state of affairs, here, in this street full of people who go about, each pursuing his own business. Whether cobbler or baker, milkman or mailman, each function can be recognized by the clothes they wear, and all the tasks are divided up among them. They have established authorities and agencies for the public order.

Not a few call themselves poets, and these describe their own profession in verse, or the moods of existence. Some others regulate men's relationship with the Supreme Being. Many know and greet each other, and all know that together they are fashioning what is called "mankind." A shiver of pride and a sublime sensation thrill them at the thought: We are this round circle which bears within itself its meaning and its law. We have an agreement that none of us will go beyond the posted limits of this enclosed park. We make ample allowances for the imperfections of our establishment, but we are also very wary of whoever would call our reality as a whole into question. For even though many a particular could be improved upon, yet, as a whole, everything is as it must be.

He had the other vision, however. He regarded them with his Father's eyes. What they characterized as imperfections was for him a horrible leprosy on the face and throughout the body—a scab and a pus-filled abscess that devoured their soul and turned them into cripples. What they called their ties were heavy, unbreakable chains which they dragged with great toil, driven on by demons. And what they praised as the cheerful moderation of their limitations, this, seen from within, was a boundless despair. An emptiness like dull hunger gaped in their souls: no expansive emptiness this, but rather a narrow, restricting hollowness that deprived them of head and senses. They walked along in an ugly nakedness, but they thought they were covered in each other's sight and had even lost the ability to feel the cold. What plagued them was so insidious that imperceptibly all of their sensations died away. They were dead, so thoroughly dead that they thought they were alive. They stood turned away from God and so far from his truth that they regarded everything as being in order. So much the prey of sin that they had no idea of what sin was. So rejected that they took themselves to be among the elect. So doomed to the abyss and the flames that they mistook the abyss for God and the flames for love.

And now there he stood, at the edge of their land. How was he to go over the border? In which language would they be able to understand his message? In what translation and disguise would his language find access to their ear? How must he conceal the radiance of eternity upon his face in order to encounter them without frightening them? But if he were to disguise himself and appear among them as one of them, then everything would be still more difficult. How could he then be told apart? How could he make them understand that he was someone else? How could he, clothed in flesh, demand from them a divine faith? O dangerous adventure, impossible undertaking! They will have to take offense at him. They will turn everything around. They will understand his sayings and discourses as a new morality and a plan to improve the world, and in his example they will see nothing but a teacher of religion. And when he raises the cloak a little and a ray from his Heart strikes them, they will be horrified and cry out "Blasphemy!" and they will pick up stones until he again conceals himself behind his mask. And last of all, in the name of world order and the fear of God, they will exterminate him for being a scandal (he seduces the people . . .) and will set him up as an example for all times to come. Let him either be a man like them or—remain a God! They will confound everything. They will chum up to him, attempting to implicate him in their circles and to manipulate him in the interest of their own will to power and perfection and their ambition for the first places. And whenever he asks for their love, and begs for their supportive nearness and warmth, then they will shrink back before him as would strangers and cast him out into a divine, into a hellish solitude.

He nonetheless wants to attempt it. He takes counsel with his Heart, which betrays to him the little joys and sufferings of their everyday life. Of these he wants to speak and in these he wants to conceal himself. And now, you humans, you wanderers—stop! Look here and consider this spectacle with me. The eternal Wisdom, which plumbs the depths of God and which, born before the morning star, ordains all worlds and their courses, all destinies and the paths of all creatures: see how the eternal Wisdom suddenly begins to stammer and to babble like a nursemaid; see how it tells little stories ("true" stories which perhaps have even happened): "There was once a man who had two sons . . . " And the children listen and clap and call out: One *more* story! "There was once a farmer who went out to sow his field . . . " A hundred such stories, and the children open wide their eyes and their mouths and find it amusing and exciting. Everything human can be used as a parable, and today, as Wisdom journeys among men as a pilgrim in disguise, all that Wisdom had once created from its seat above the stars becomes a stool for it to climb upon and make its voice heard.

Thus does the Stranger proceed, and into his tales he introduces heaven knows what strange-sounding note in order to make them perk up and listen: a scent and a taste from the world that is their home; a wind blowing through it all and which one hears, not knowing whence it comes or where it goes. Something had to touch them and bring to memory things long forgotten. An invisible, gentle arrow had to wound them in an unsuspected place. Through the miserable rattling of human words something like a distant music from Paradise had to resound and make the sails of their souls swell up with anticipation.

But they have ears and yet they hear not, an understanding and yet understand not. All of their senses are shut off to the real world. They are incapable of interpreting not only his words, but even his actions and gestures. Only within their own circles can they bring order to an event: they explain it by lowering it to their own level. They can grasp something new only by understanding it as a part of their old store. They are like cattle that see and eat only the grass that agrees with their belly. The Prince of this world still

63

holds them by his leash, having cast a veil over their eyes. And when this Prince distributes bread among them in the wilderness, then they vaguely believe that they have scented their Master. They trot after him like a herd of goats in the mountains when they smell salt and sweat. And he will have to flee and hide himself from them to be rid of the greed of their impulses. But their shepherds are already on the alert and extreme mistrust has perked up their ears. They have scented the Arch-enemy and they will not rest until he has succumbed to their blows.

No: speeches and deeds will not do it. He must first fashion the eyes which can see him; he must implant in them nonexistent ears, that they may hear; an unknown sense of touch, that they may feel God, new senses of smell and taste that they may smell God's fragrance and savor his fare. He must make their whole spirit new, new from its very foundations. But the price for this will be an exorbitant one: he will have to take their dead, dull senses upon himself and lose his Father and the whole heavenly world. In death, in hell, his pregnant Heart will have to dissolve and—now as a wholly ruined Heart which has melted into a shapeless sea—he will give himself to them as their drink: the love-potion which will at last bewitch their all-too-sober hearts.

The Heart of the World must first create his world for himself. The Head of the World must himself fashion his own Body. Until now a law had held good in the world: love is awakened by what is beautiful, by what pleases us, by what does not appear unworthy of our love. The fire of sublime empathy is enkindled and nourished by every noble feature of the beloved. Human affection advances over the bridge of innate worth. In the long run, love would die if it were not nourished by the exchange of self-giving. So Nature wills it, for God has bestowed great gifts on his children that they may be pleasing to one another.

But what do God and sin have in common? What kind of sympathy would want to mediate between light and darkness? From nothing had his word once created the world; from less than nothing—from hatred—must he produce the world of grace a second time. Must strike water from a rock. He himself must invent whatever is to be love-worthy, worthy of his love. He himself must provide not only the love, but the return of love. In the power of the Word he must also bestow the power of response. He has no "thou" in which he might lose himself; in his solitude he produces love's counterpart. He lets the darkness enter into his flames; he lets the world, which neither knows nor wants him, become his very Body. And from the solitude of the one Body he creates his Bride.

It is as if the sun were rising over the chaos, bringing to light a world of only desert, ice and rock. No animal in sight, no living thing: no forest, no blade of grass, no seed, not a single footprint nor the slightest possibility of life. And over this death the Light of the World shines forth. It shines and shines, bringing forth day after day from its storehouse. With calm equanimity it rises and sets, letting its life flow forth—a life which was the light of men—until one day the marvel happens and a first timid tip peers up from the ground, then a second, then Twelve and Seventy-two. Until from the first seed's grace-filled death, a narrow patch of fruitland at length begins to take shape. The first bush, the first shadow darkens, the blossoming winds grow animated. The rivers surround themselves with greenery; and at last, when the carpet has spread in all its unbroken beauty, Man the King appears and casts a thankful glance up to the motherly light which has begotten him.

But who is this sun? Who has so overburdened himself with this hard-labor of love? Who is the light which illumines every man who comes into this world? It is a Heart like ours, a human Heart, which itself thirsts for a return of love. A Heart like other hearts, full of warm folly, full of imprudent hope: full of obstinacy. A Heart that pines away when it is not loved. Who can live his whole life among nothing but enemies? And if one of us should be cast like Robinson Crusoe on an empty island, we would still have the memory of our youth and would nourish our solitude with the images of long-past friendship. A human heart is not like God: it does not revolve upon itself; it is not without its needs. It beats, it pulses, it searches, it requires alien blood in order to live. A human heart is not, like God, almighty. It cannot, in lordly fashion, create with a word. God spoke: "Let it

66

be!'' And it was. What can a heart do if it does not receive love in return? What will it do if we do not want to love?

It will all be more difficult than it had appeared when considered from heaven. Seen from there, love was simply irresistible, always accustomed to victory. Man had only to be approached with a full cup and already those parched with thirst would kneel and beg for a drink. They would have to feel the nearness of salvation: how could they help it? With this certainty had he come. And now that he stands there clothed in dull flesh, in his breast this Heart of flesh pounding—how strange, how different everything is from what he had expected! How greatly this garment obscures the divine ray!

And how careful he will have to be! How soft, how hesitant his steps will have to be if men are not to stumble against his love and misunderstand it! For they will perceive the great warmth of his Heart and stretch out their arms to embrace him. But such is not the love which he intends, and out of love he will have to withdraw from them, will have to feign coldness and do violence to his own Heart. And it will be even more difficult to have not only to give but to teach his own love to those whom he loves, to school them mercilessly in the same mercy, to cast them out into a solitude as deadly as his own. With his own hand he will have to thrust seven swords into the heart of the most beloved of mortals. Deliberately and intentionally he will have to let his friend die (this was

67

bitter enough to him). And those whom he had with great effort gathered into his fold he will send out unprotected, like young lambs among wolves. He must not only chastise everyone whom he loves in order to school him in discipline, but harrow him to initiate him into the mystery of the new love.

By one Heart's solitude was the world redeemed. Not by the lovely solitude of the hermitage, which is erected around life's scars as a protection and a barrier, but by that other solitude which abandons us defenseless to the tumult. By a solitude in which the heart—softly tossed about in the icy water of impossibilities—is to experience love as the cold blade of a sword and as an ever-wakeful wound. The people are stolid, animal-like; the priests lie in wait for him; the disciples are obdurate and fight over the first places; one of the Twelve will betray him. In his country and in his native city, and even in his very home, the Prophet encounters only distrust. His cousins take him for mad. To strike him down, children are murdered. He is cast here and there because no position on his hard bed is bearable. Now he storms forth and wants to force them to love. He threatens them with eternal death if they do not eat his Body, and he reveals himself to the three loved ones in the enraptured splendor of his native glory. But already he hastens to return from glory so that they will not love him out of compulsion, and no one may build himself a hut within his heavenly light. Turn where he may, they will always be annoyed.

Like a potter who models his pot on the revolving wheel, he transforms his Heart to offer it to men in new and different ways. To no avail; they take no notice. They already know it all. They have weighed him and found him to be too heavy. How light their love is: quickly perceived, airily engaged in, simple as sleeping and eating. To what purpose the unprecedented and exorbitant demand, the dizzying dance on the tightrope, the spirit dislocated, the right measure disturbed? They reject him, and he wanders among them as a stranger. Amid his own world, God learned to be what he had been eternally: alone and one. By solitude did he redeem the world.

However, solitude is not yet abandonment. For the sun, too, is alone in heaven. But what if it should go down into darkness, if it itself should perish? Every heart lives on hope. Only hope wards off the vertigo on the air-woven hanging-bridge of time, swaying from second to second over the abyss of non-existence.

The heart beats. To what end? For tomorrow, for more beautiful mornings, and the even road seems always to rise before our gaze. Thy Kingdom come. Very near has the Kingdom of Heaven come. Yet a little while, my children . . . Up to now loyal friends have been scarce. But hope and press on, my Heart; the others will not forever oppose you. "Simon, do you see that woman?" It sounds almost like triumph. What was accomplished today—the shattering of the bitter vessel and the outpouring of fragrance and of tears—this will also happen to you one day, O Pharisee, though perhaps quite late. The hope of God's Heart! The Kingdom of God is like a grain of mustard which (this is said with a mysterious smile) is smaller than all the seeds of the garden . . . And in his spirit he sees the Tree which has grown out of his Heart, and in whose branches the angels of heaven nestle. Its crown rustles high in the sun, in the wind of the Father.

But then his gaze is lowered to the earth, and he awakens as from a distant dream. Where is the Kingdom? And who belongs to it? Which one of these Twelve, of these Seventy-two, is worthy to cross the threshold? And where are they, the others, the innumerable, whom the Father entrusted to him? Has the Kingdom at all grown since the days of his baptism in the Jordan? Have not the throngs fallen away from him in the hour of great promise? Will not the Twelve also betray him? Will the Kingdom not slip away between his fingers like a fleeting dream? By what magic, then, is it supposed to come? How am I to bring it about? How can one single Heart suffice to transform hell into Paradise? And I cannot say: Father, *you* create the Kingdom!, for you have entrusted that task to me and you have laden the world upon my shoulders. Hope! In what? Not in men, and not in time, and also not in God . . . Hope: but in what? In myself? In the power of my love? But will it hold out to the end? What if it should fail? If on the Cross I must acknowledge that all has been in vain?

And the Kingdom is swallowed up in the night and my Heart breaks in two with a great cry because it cannot go on, because the power of God by which it beat—beat in hope—was withdrawn from it? And when the last drop of water and blood has escaped from my Heart and its gaping void stares up to heaven, what if then the imperious command of the angry Judge should blaze against me with terrible threats?

Hard the task, but harder still the failure. Harder the experience of impotence and the certitude of the end. The flower of grace is so implausible that it grows only from the hardest stone of the impossible. Grace is bestowed gratuitously and the risk of this gift's freedom must be suffered to the end. For in the end everything runs the risk, the world as much as grace. When God forgives, his forgiving is a giving away. For what love is not prodigality itself?

This is why the sun must be extinguished and God's Heart must fail. This Heart was to be so strong that it would not recoil from utter weakness. Like a leaking boat it begins to let in water, and no cry for help will save it from sinking. For God's Wisdom had resolved to triumph by perishing, and thus it poured itself out in sheer folly. It is foolish to die for a lost cause. It is foolish to hope when everything has long been played out. Foolish did God's love become, and wholly without dignity.

And now he sets his foot into the bottomless morass of the world, into the swamp of sin. The

71

waves of temptation spray up around him: The Kingdom might still be saved! Believe in your power! Trust the star of the Magi! Have the legions of angels carry you off over the void! Work the miracle that will bind their heart to you: give them bread and circus! Bend the knee of your rash Heart (it is good to kneel!) and adore me! "Father!", cries the Heart in its vertiginous plunge, "into your hands—which I do not feel, which opened to let me fall, which will catch me at the bottom of the abyss—into your hands I entrust my Spirit. Into your hands I breathe out my Spirit. My Holy Spirit."

The Heart became Spirit, and from the travails of the Spirit the New World was born. A great roar filled the house, windows and doors flew open, and eyes and ears as well. The heavy armor was burst open from within and the cover removed from the face. This Heart's love loved even to annihilation, and since it had become invisible in itself, it now emerged in the hearts of the redeemed. Once it had been one sun, alone in the cold night of the world; now the light is scattered in a firmament of stars. It had seemed to struggle with the darkness, had seemed to sink down into the mire, overcome by the chaos; but no enemy is mightier and no night more night-filled than the radiant darkness of love.

CHAPTER IV

THE FATHER'S VINEYARD

I AM THE VINE, you are the branches. I am the root, the trunk and the bough, inconspicuous, cut back and stunted, half-covered by the ground, under snow and shale. But you are my blossoms, you my fruit. During long winter nights I gather up my power. Out of the dry rubble of barren earth I suck up the tasteless water, drop by drop. But under the action of the year's storms and the blasts of the sun I send out shoot after shoot; I sweat my precious blood, my golden wine. This blood this wine: this is you. I am the vine, you are the wine I have wept. Tendrils at first, succulent and supple as snakes, you shoot out. Greedy for life, for freedom, you crave to escape the barky trunk and try out an independent existence, and you stretch out in the sun for sheer love of life. You hold out long, prehensile arms to grasp, to snatch, to fetter, to bind to yourselves anything alive with movement. You call it knowledge and love. The intertwining tendrils curl up to heaven, up towards the light and the stars, greedily grasping for God, but all they seize with the crooked fingers is air and nothingness.

I am the vine, and I myself have partaken of this craving drive, for summer presses hard on spring and wisdom grows from disillusionment. My Father is the vine-dresser and he prunes away every branch in me that does not bear fruit. Under the cutting knife, the tendrils' wild eagerness falls to the ground. Once again I stand bare; the greater part of you withers and is destined for the fire. Burning, the blade cuts through your greed for world and God. Struck at the root, it collapses with a powerless flicker; what still appears to be ordinary life is but the glow of death, which scorches and consumes branch after branch. Allow this fire to burn in your members, for you burn in me and for me. To me has all judgment been entrusted, and no one comes to me unless it is through fire. And the covetous will not enter the Kingdom of Heaven.

Leaves, too, grow from the trunk, succulent and shiny, and the sap makes them swell to the appointed size. At the peak of summer they unfurl, having become viscous and dark. Through them the tree breathes. Beautifully structured, with sharp and precise borders, they deploy their nature, similar to one another and yet no two the same. Their faces to the sun, they drink in the light and convey a quickening warmth to the trunk. All strive toward the brightness, and although they provide much shade they always stretch out in such a way that each of them receives its draft of light. And, to be sure, the trunk also is dependent on the foliage, and as long as summer lasts it is the leaves which appear to be its fruit. There are many beings in the world, and a gladsome impulse of surging expansion permeates your nature. Without nature, no fruit at all could be gathered into the celestial barns. But look: God's sun is hard; August burns like a glowing oven, and for weeks now no rain has fallen. The trunk no longer has any moisture to give its greenery. Then it is that a shudder goes through all the leaves: they know they have been sacrificed. This time no knife will be needed; wise nature herself erects a small impenetrable layer between the bough and the stalk. So it is that slow autumn sets in with its coolness, and soon with its frosts, and the interplay of red and yellow on the leaves is like an illumining portrait of lost love, like the idea of the summer which is past. Remembrance: the interior mirror of what no longer is, the eye of life turned within. Let it blow, leaf, and do not cling to the branch. You are but the garment and not the body. And each harvest is a feast of death. See: I myself, the vine, shake from me the superfluous burden. Let your own reality now go its way, and think of the fruit.

I also bear blossoms, insignificant ones, not to be compared with the great flowers of the earth. And yet the bees and the drones found them, hiding under the leaves. Having coupled in silence they now await their hour. And while all around the mowed meadow turns to yellow, the grapes swell up to bursting. Still for a long while they will be unripe, sour and tough. Have patience, my grapes, it is I who will bear you to term. At first you did not seem much more than tiny acrid skins, hanging underexposed in the shade of the leaves—a scared little crew. You did not yet believe in me, and you worriedly conjectured how you would nourish yourselves with the scarce rain and deprived of the sun. And you did not know that all power wells up from within, from me. Without me you can do nothing. I do not say "little"; I say "nothing." But whoever remains in me and I remain in him, he is the one who brings in much fruit. I myself bring forth fruit in him, and he is the fruit. It is just in this that my Father is glorified: that you bring in much fruit.

Why do you rush on to deed and achievement? I am the vine; it is I who achieve. What is your deed if it is not to ripen? Let my sap rise up within you that you may hang heavy and golden. Then will the chaotic dream of deeds dreamt by the shoots in the springtime, then will the leaves' proud summer craze, then will all earth's work become ripe within your little taut spheres. You can bear in yourselves the meaning of the earth, but only through me. And when in the bowers of heaven this wine is served up at the Lamb's marriage-feast, then the whole world will be borne within it—as spirit. Then one will be able to taste on which hillside and in what year of salvation it grew, will be able to savor in it the whole landscape of its origin, and not the least of your joys will be lost. But everything about it has invisibly turned within, and the dividing borderlines between being and being are dissolved in the unifying tide, and all bubbling eagerness has ceased fermenting, and all sadness has resurrected into brightness.

I am the Resurrection and the Life, but not as the world knows them: that decaying cycle of springs and autumns, that millstone of melancholy, that aping of eternal life. All the world's living and dying, taken together, are one great death, and it is this death that I awaken to life. Once I entered the world, a new and unknown sap began to circulate in the veins and branches of nature. The powers of destiny, the might of the planets, the demons of the blood, the rulers of the air, the spirit of the earth, and whatever other dark things still cower in the secret folds of creation: all of this has now been subdued and is ordered about and must obey the higher law. All the world's form is to me but matter that I inspirit. My action is not grafted from without to the old life, to the old pleasure-gardens of Pan; being the very Life of life, I transform the marrow from within. All that dies becomes the property of my life. All that passes over into autumn runs ashore on my spring. All that turns to mould fertilizes my blossoms. All that denies has already been convicted; all that covets has already been dispossessed; all that stiffens has already been broken.

I am not one of the resurrected; I am the Resurrection itself. Whoever lives in me, whoever is taken up into me, is taken up in resurrection. I am the transformation. As bread and wine are transformed, so the world is transformed into me. The grain of mustard is tiny, and yet its inner might does not rest until it overshadows all the world's plants. Neither does my resurrection rest until the grave of the last soul has burst, and my powers have reached even to the furthest branch of creation. You see death; you feel the descent to the end. But death is itself a life, perhaps the most living life; it is the darkening depth of my life, and the end is itself the beginning, and the descent is itself the soaring up.

What can still be called death after I have died my death? Does not every dying from now on receive the meaning and the seal of my death? Is its significance not that of a stretching out of the arms and a perfect sacrifice into the bosom of my Father? In death the barriers fall away; in death the ever-forbidden lock snaps open; the sluice bursts, the waters pour out freely. All the terrors that hover around death are morning mists that disperse into the blue. Even the slow death of souls when they bitterly shut themselves off from God—when they entrench and wall themselves up, when the world towers up around them like the pit of a grave, and all love becomes as the smell of mould, and hope withers, and a cold defiance rears its head and shows its tongue, a viper up from the depths: have I not suffered my way through all these deaths? And what can their poison do against the deadly antidote of my love? Every horror became for my love a garment in which to conceal itself, a wall through which to walk.

Do not be afraid of death. Death is the liberating flame of the sacrifice, and sacrifice is transformation. But (eucharistic) transformation is communion in my eternal life. I am Life. Whoever believes in me, whoever eats and drinks me, has life in himself, eternal life, already here and now, and I will raise him up on the last day. Do you grasp this mystery? You live, work, suffer; and yet, it is not you: it is another who lives, works and suffers in you. You are the ripening fruit, but what brings the ripening about, what ripens: it is I who am that. I am the power, the fullness, that sheds itself into your emptiness, filling it up. But by filling, the fullness fulfills itself in the emptiness, and thus you are also my fullness. You need me, for without me you can do nothing, and I need you (though I need no creature at all) in order to reveal my fullness by its outpouring. Thus do I live in you, and you live in me. I am the grain of seed that falls into your furrow and dies, and when I rise up from your ground it is your seed that emerges. And, again, you are the grain of wheat that falls into God's furrow and dies through baptism and crucifixion, and when you rise up you are my harvest. Two lives become visible, and yet they are but one. For in the ear of wheat one cannot distinguish what derives from the field and what has been provided by the plant's own power. The raw material is always the same, only brought together in new ways by the combinations of organic life, and, to the very marrow of Being, this material has become still more noble. So it is that you live, but no longer you: rather, it is I who live in you. For this reason you are my possession, my fruit, my branches. But I too am your possession, for I have given myself to you as your captive, and I stand at your disposal as your own inner being. You no longer belong to yourselves; you have become the Temple of God. Nor do I any longer belong to myself: I have become the quarry for the Temple of Mankind.

I am the vine, you are the branches. You have blossomed forth from me. Are you then surprised if a drop of my Heart's blood trickles into your every thought and deed? Are you surprised if the thoughts of my Heart quietly infiltrate your worldly heart? If a whispering takes wing in you and day and night you perceive a low, beckoning call? To a love that wants to suffer, to a love that, together with mine, redeems? Are you surprised if the desire comes upon you to risk your life and all your strength and put them in jeopardy for your brothers? And to complete in your own body what is still lacking to my sufferings, what must still lack as long as I have not suffered my Passion in all my branches and members? For, to be sure, none of you is redeemed by anyone save myself; but I am the total Redeemer only united with each of you. Do you want to accomplish the great change with me and build up the Father's Kingdom? Do you want to live my mind, the resolve of one who did not hold on to his form of God convulsively and clutchingly, but who broke it and emptied it out so that it began to flow as the courage to serve and as lowliness, became obedient even unto death on the Cross? Are you willing? For my work must be perfected in you and it will be brought to term only when my Heart beats in yours, only when all hearts, now submissive and docile, beat for the Father together in my Heart. Are you willing? No, you are not yet willing. You still beg off. You still leave me in the lurch. You still think: "HE is the Redeemer, not I!" It is true, I am, and will go on bleeding and atoning until you grasp it. And, even as you struggle against me, you have already fallen to me in the midst of your self-defense. Your solitude will weep for me and your rotting defiance will acknowledge me.

Is it now through you, my branches, that I die? Have I not become weak in order to strengthen you? Have I not long ago suffered the empty solitude in which you entrench yourselves? And when you burn down to gray ash, dying out to no avail as something which cannot be salvaged, will I not then be victor? Have I not already triumphed? Is the sword with which you pierced my side not the same as the one which comes out of my mouth and divides like a living fire, penetrating between spirit and soul, joints and marrow? Am I not the magnet which draws all things to itself, even the nails from ships' hulls, that they may sink into me? Too long already has my grace been flowing into your hollow vessels, still you let it lie empty within you, still now does your womb avoid my seed, O Jerusalem, my Bride: still do you behave like a whore. But see: the weakness with which you weaken me can no longer be an obstacle. When I am weak, then I am strong. Let yourself be weakened by my weakness, my Bride, that the fruit of your body may grow within you, the child of our love. How much longer will you insist on my making up for your refusals by my suffering? How much longer will you shift the burden onto my shoulders, a burden which, if borne by both of us, would become the delight of the Kingdom of Heaven? What branch refuses the sap which the roots have gathered up with much toil and which finally offers itself after being coaxed up long channels? Or should I be like the rubber tree, which is slit and then sweats out its blood into little attached containers? For how long will you separate my solitude from yours, instead of allowing them to come together in the oneness of one single love? A solitude that loves bears fruit; a resistant solitude, even if it suffers, wards off all fruit.

Do not take offense, you branches, at the deformity of your trunk. Do not scorn the powerlessness that strengthens you. For in me death is at work, but in you, life. You are sated, you have already become rich; without me you have attained to lordship. Were it only true lordship, then could I reign in you! But while you are strong, I am still weak; and at the same time as you make a show of your honors, I am despised. To this very hour I suffer hunger and thirst, nakedness and blows. I am the homeless one who slaves away at the work of his hands. I am the accused one who blesses, the persecuted who bears it patiently, the slandered consoler, the world's refuse. Still today, as always, I am the draining dishwater in which you all wash. And just as you despise me, so you despise my disciples and emissaries, for in them also the same law of weakness is at work. And because all life has its origin in impotence and even in disgrace, I have appointed the last place for them, as if they were evildoers condemned to death. But just as I live from the power of God after being crucified in weakness, so too will they prove themselves to you to be alive in me with the power of God. For look: in them my life has begun to circulate and to bring them to ripeness as my firstfruits. Just as the strawberry plant sends out long shoots which soon form roots and finally produce a new plant, so too have I multiplied my inner center and established new centers in hearts sprung from mine. My children become fathers and new communities blossom from the blood of my Apostles' hearts. For my grace is always fruitful, and my gift it is for you to pass my grace on. My treasure is to be found in prodigality, and only he possesses me who gives me away. For I am indeed the Word, and how can one possess a word other than by speaking it?

I am the Head, you are the members. Whatever I think and plan you are to show forth and do. Through you, my hands and feet, I intend to transform and transfigure the world. The plan is invisible in the brain, but the body makes it take shape in successive stages. When I, a man among many, unobtrusively walked through the hamlets of Judea, who had any inkling of what I was? That man was but the seed of myself, not yet even been born. For the travail of my birth began at the Cross, and rising up I, the Light of the World, came into the light of the world. Becoming invisible in my Ascension, I entered the world as its soul and spirit, and, growing in youth and wisdom in men's souls and spirits, I began to manifest my fullness. And I will give you a share of the riches of my glory that through my spirit you may grow strong in might according to the interior man that I may dwell in your hearts through faith, and that you, rooted and immersed in love, may together with all the saints, plumb my breadth and length, my height and depth, having become as clear air for the rays of my love, a love that transcends every concept, so that at last God's fullness may fill you to overflowing. Thus will my Body be perfected in its members' ministering to one another, until together we all grow unto my perfect and completed manhood, unto the mature shape of my masculine Body.

And now, before I depart from you as an individual man who goes where you cannot follow (into your souls' innermost abode), before I rise up in you with my thousandfold voice—a voice that will be your voice, the voice of the Church's choir—I want to raise my individual voice one last time as this one man, and I pray to the Father:

Father, the hour is here. Glorify your Son that your Son may glorify you! Let me descend into death and let my veins gush forth. Allow my Heart to grow wide, great as the world's bounds, by dying a death that is greater than life. Allow me to manifest in gestures of earthly suffering the glory of our love, a glory which you bestowed on me in the beginning, before the world came to be, ever since my Being was born from you. Do not refuse me this request of being allowed to reveal you in the terrors of hell and even in the very form of sin, so that you too may be glorified through me in these, my members and branches. For henceforth we—they and I—are one indistinguishable unity. Earlier on, Father, you and I were one, and they stood outside of us as enemies, and from a distance we took counsel to see how they might be helped. Today I stand in the midst of our enemies; I have become a traitor to your justice, and if you want to strike out at them, strike first at me. I cover them like the hen protects her chicks. I take their place. I consecrate myself wholly to them: I catch the lightning-bolt which is destined for them and which you are already preparing in your storm-pregnant stillness. I rob from your Olympus the fire with which you kill me in order to forge with it the jewel which is the Church. I forge the arrow of your justice into the scepter of your mercy. For, O my Father! What else is your justice than your love for me, and what the wrathful glance of your eye other than the most glorious revelation of your love for me? It is not I who am the lover: it is you, and all that is mine is yours. And so look: even your enemies here, my friends, are yours. And I do not place myself as a protective wall before them to shield them from your fury. Rather, I take them into my hand like the celebrant takes his paten and I raise them up to you. They are yours because they are mine, and all that is mine is yours. They are yours; you have entrusted them to me and they have kept your Word. For I have given to them the words which you gave to me, and they have accepted them. And they have believed and understood that I came forth from you, for my Word is in them, I myself am in them, one with them, just as you, Father, and I are one single One. And when I now go and sacrifice myself for them, to whom should I entrust them if not to you, Father, as my precious inheritance, as my Incarnation's fruit of sorrows and as the grapes on my vine? For whom have I ripened them if not for you, so that, once I have conquered death and hell, I might place them on your eternal table in the perfected vessel of the King-dom? They are yours: protect them from the Evil One. And because they are now indeed a part of my-self and my destiny has not remained foreign to them, and because I consecrate and sacrifice myself for the world in the mystery of vicarious atonement, for these reasons I say yet this: Consecrate them to the Truth! As you have sent me into the world, so too have I sent them out into the world. Sacrifice them also in their mission that, as rays of the light, they

86

may shed light as they go down into the darkness and, as they themselves are consumed, they may brighten the darkness. Partaking in my mission from you, they will go out from me, and as they wander forth, beaming my light and expending themselves, they will realize their unity with me and realize my unity with you. They will experience what our love is, a love which does not clutch to itself but which ventures separation, throwing even the utmost forsakenness into the gamble. For you, Father, are now going to let go of me. And before I no longer know it because of the night which will soon overtake me, I want to tell you this for the last time: in this night I recognize your highest love, and do not wish it to be otherwise (your will be done!). In the freedom with which you now cast me out I adore your divine right, and I kiss the finger that shows me the way out, that they too, believing and not feeling, may in the night of the spirit come to perceive our Spirit as it blows. May they be one as we are one, and in no other way. May I be in them as you are in me, and in no other way. Salvation lies only in your Cross, and consolation lies in being forsaken by you, and graces flow from the open side of the pierced Heart.

Thus do I blossom before you, Father, and for you I bear the world's vine-branches. You recognize the life that flows in my boughs: it is your own life with me. What flows down into me vertically from you, my Source, this have I spread far and wide horizontally over the earth's expanse. And what was our eternal life, shared by both of us horizontally, up above in the circle of eternity, this have I brought down vertically to the very depths of the earth. This is why I, as the Mediator, have the shape of the Cross. The Cross is within me, and I will carry it because, in virtue of your mandate, I am what I am. I am the Cross, and whoever is in me cannot escape the cross. Love itself has the shape of the cross for in love all roads cross. For this reason, Father, you have given man the form of the cross when he extends his arms in love, so that the world, judged in the sign of the Son of Man, may through this judgment be directed towards you and be saved.

PART TWO

THE SUFFERING

CHAPTER V

THE PUTTING-OFF GAME

I DON'T WANT TO. I know I should, but I don't want to. I'll pretend I'm deaf; I'll curl up and show my bristles. Let him touch me who dares! The arrow of the Call, sharply aimed, ricochets off. My skin is thick and weather-proofed. The Demand slides from it like water from a duck's feathers. I stand on my rights, bestowed on me from the highest source in virtue of the nature which I have received, which I am, in virtue of the instincts and habits which are implanted in me and which strive for life and development. Let no one contest these my rights, not even the highest authority! And even if someone should dare, let him know that I don't want to do it.

Soft it approaches, almost inaudible and yet quite unavoidable: a ray of light, an offer of power, a command that is more and less than a command—a wish, a request, an invitation, an enticement: brief as an instant, simple to grasp as the glance of two eyes. It contains a promise: love, delight and a vision extending over an immense and vertiginous distance. Liberation from the unbearable dungeon of my ego.

91

The adventure I had always longed for. The perfect feat of daring in which I am sure to win all only by losing all. The source of life opening up inexhaustibly to me, who am dying of thirst! The gaze is perfectly tranquil, having nothing of magical power or of hypnotic compulsion: a questioning gaze which allows me my freedom. At the bottom of it, the shadows of affliction and of hope alternate.

I lower my eyes; I look to the side. I don't want to say "no" in the face of those eyes. I give them time to turn away, time to withdraw into their cave of eternity, time to grow dark, to be blurred. I am not at home: "The master says he cannot see you at the moment." I give those eyes time to disappear again behind their heavy lid, the curtain of eternity. For a second, precisely at the moment when I know it is too late, a nameless sorrow makes me tremble: happiness has been forfeited, love mocked, and no one can bring them back to me! The prison door thuds into its lock: again I am a prisoner in what is to me so dear and so hated—myself.

Disposed of. Once again disposed of. You hold yourself back to the point that it has to slip away. Happy to be alone once more—no, somehow not really alone. Alone with a burden, a pressure that mounts, becomes unbearable, has to be disposed of as quickly as possible. I look around me frantically: where can this burden be shifted? It's most urgent; it's crushing me utterly; I have only one thought: away with it! And I push it off on the first passerby. Twice rejected, twice disposed of. And yet really only once.

92

The one disposed of is the one on whom I pushed it off. He is stuck with it. With one stroke I dispose of both things—grace and guilt. Because I did not want to bear the burden of grace, I excused myself of the burden of guilt.

"Adam, where are you? Adam, what have you done?"

"I am not to blame: it was the woman who seduced me."

"Woman, what have you done?"

"It was the serpent who seduced me."

"O humankind, what have you done?"

"It was your creation, Lord, the beauty you have given to nature, the poison in blossoming flowers, the thorn in the rose, the insect in the flower . . . "

"Cain, what have you done?"

"Am I my brother's keeper? Am I the keeper of my blood?"

Appeal to the universal. To the course of events. To habit. So it is with all of them. "After all, I'm only another human being." *Ecce Homo*. I push it off on "Man."

Life is realistic; it always vindicates the sober. To be sure, the "ghostly hour" is there, too, the hour when strange things touch you, when something brushes by your face like the down of a nightbird in the darkness. You shudder and are startled. Your soul's hair stands on end in the wake of this unspeakable and abrupt encounter. And so, such a way out is still a possibility, this imaginary door, this enchanted pathway and invisible bridge over the abyss, of which I dreamt as both child and youth—the road in which I believed and for which I hoped with such frenzy. So it still is possible . . . even now, even today! Then I haven't yet been abandoned, haven't yet been given up as hopeless . . . I'm being inquired after; my presence is desired, needed even—or so it seems. Somewhere there exists a bright image of me, an image of what I could have been, of what I am still (but how?) capable of becoming. But these "ghostly hours" recur more and more seldom, and the enveloping layers of everyday life grow stronger and thicker around me, and gradually the husk turns to flesh and the flesh to husk. I seal myself off to God and this becomes my usual state—my second nature. Maybe this is the habit of sin, the habit of evil. And when the reeking refuse crowds in around me more and more so that it chokes me, this habit will arouse a nausea in me and then grace-filled nature will give me the urge and the possibility of vomiting up my guilty soul before God. But perhaps what is also involved is the habit of an innocuous life, the drudgery of ordered existence which requires as its spice a drop of resignation, or the sing-song of a quieted conscience which requires a residue of bad conscience in order to weigh down its keel in the passage through the deep. God is truly forbearance, God is truly grace. God will not expect from me any more than he expects from others. I am a person who thinks ethically. I have murdered no one, broken into no bank, set no houses on fire, never been convicted before. I am a man like other men,

94

perhaps even a little better than many. This will certainly be shown at the Judgment: nothing very incriminating will be produced against me. God knows well enough what a good will I've had. I've exerted myself in providing for and rearing my family, as is only right. Day and night I've taken care that those I'm responsible for should lack nothing. I've washed, cooked, done the shopping, sewn, ironed, made savings, stored supplies, thought of the future. By and large we've enjoyed heaven's blessings. There was always plenty of food, and on Sundays we took our well-deserved recreation. Even then, these last years, we've had our retirement income. No, I really don't know what else . . . Oh, yes, let me not forget this: I've also been a person who's fulfilled his religious obligations. I am a practicing Christian. I am a good Catholic. Sundays I've always been in church. I've made my Easter duty. I've paid my tithes. I've given alms. I've always said my morning and evening prayers. I have often been to confession and they've always been valid. I have made the nine First Fridays (which, after all, give me a kind of insurance before God, sanctioned by the Church). I've gone to Communion every Sunday. I've communicated daily.

"I have, I have." What I've done with my religion is raise up walls against God. By my practices I have stopped up my ears to God's call. Quietly, imperceptibly, everything which could have been life has become a mechanism behind which my soul has laid itself to rest. Life is so long, and the constant repetition of the same thing causes such lethargy. If you live near a waterfall, after a week you'll no longer hear its rumble. In the same way, we have forgotten how to listen. The spheres make music, but all we hear any more is ourselves and the clatter of our own interests. More and more cracks are filled in and the stilling of the divine call becomes more and more a matter of course. It is walled up, mortared within the system of life we've invented. Just as during the day we allow the caged bird to sing and at night we cover him up, so from time to time I take a fancy to listen to God's Word play a tune. This can take the form of a sermon, an edifying Bible hour, or perhaps a performance of St. Matthew's Passion, a poem by Rilke, a vague feeling of the sacred before a landscape. Always enjoyed in the context of a comfort which is expensive enough as it is, these solemn moments of life are quite sufficient for my religious needs—which in any event are so muffled that I hardly need to cover the cage any more. Under the weight of my good conscience and under the ample bottom of my great heart, the voice of Truth has been stifled. It's been silent for a long time now.

Or I can postpone guilt until tomorrow. The eye that looks at me fixedly always says "today." "It is now that I want to be loved." But I lower my eyes and say: "I will love you tomorrow. Tomorrow you'll see what I'm capable of doing for you. You'll see the sacrifices I'll bring to you. Tomorrow I'll pay you twice over if you'll only grant me this one hour today. I must yet pluck the rose before it fades away, but the rosehips I'll bring you for sure. Give me the spring and I'll let you have the autumn, maybe even late summer. Just for today turn away your gaze, and starting tomorrow you'll be able to look at me all you like." "I'm coming now, I'm coming right away!" the child cries up to his mother when she calls him in, and he finishes playing his game, thinking that surely obedience includes a certain period of grace—a human margin. Who could all at once make a clean break with his life? Why, God, do you want to jump steps in my case? You want the whole thing all at once: one's whole heart, whole soul, whole mind—all my strength; and yet, gradual development is the very law of life. As a good pedagogue, you too ought to abide by this law. I'm willing to turn over a fourth to you now, and when I'm thirty a half, and so, little by little, you're sure to acquire the whole. Were I to tear myself away violently from everything that has grown as one with me—grown into my very heart—surely I would bleed, bleed even to death, and then you'd have only a dead man in your arms. Or, if I survived I would look back, harkening after what I had only externally overcome. Wait, then, until I've had my fill. And when at last I have the tasteless core between my teeth, then I will finally spit it out. Be patient, until the wave that now buoys me high has become a hollow valley, until the veil that now softly and enticingly envelops me has been torn and the bitter dregs of existence rise up to my eyes. We hear it said that you are primarily to be found in disappointment, in disillusionment, on life's dark side. Pass me by today and knock again when you make your next round, because by then I'll have advanced a bit. I'm not saying you should give up on me, I swear I'm not. Always draw me, but draw me gently. Catch me like a fish if you must, but without my realizing it, in the same way as time imperceptibly transforms us from lads into old men. Fondle me into your arms, just as a mother lifts her sleeping child from its crib. And if I must nevertheless feel the pain of separation, then at least yield on this point and make me this one concession: you may take me tomorrow if you'll only let me have today. I am even prepared to take up your cross, to follow your Way of the Cross station after station to the end, to the complete sacrifice and the definitive death—under one condition, that is: let it be tomorrow. I'll even stop up my ears and already today, in the midst of my pleasure, think of it and keep it clearly before my eyes: that tomorrow I will follow you. I want to think of you as the condemned man thinks of the morrow with each bite of his last meal before his execution. I want to think of you with the resolution of giving myself to you. But tomorrow, tomorrow, not today.

And, furthermore, I could offer you so much. Why do you demand so little? Why do you want this small, pitiable, good-for-nothing heart? Can't you see all the other things I could give you besides? "I'll give you half of my kingdom." Don't you perhaps want my fortune instead? Or my health? Or can I satisfy you with a vow? A certain prayer, recited daily? Do you like this novena? And how does this precious stone suit you, or that crystal? If you hold it this way you can see how it sparkles. I can show you expensive materials, embroideries and brocades, the fragrance of sacrifices, all manner of renunciations and the choicest mortifications. See how the merchandise is piled high on my display table. All of it is yours, and, so as not to seem to be stingy, I will give you many another thing besides. I would like to be particularly devoted to your Heart, "which has suffered so much for us." I would like to pray and do penance for the conversion of sinners and of hardened hearts. You have a hard time of it, don't you? The times are hard! The masses have fallen away. And even your Church . . . ! All right: I'll see what I can do for you. But you must excuse me right now, because I have to go. And the heart which lies buried under all the rubbish I have strewn about, the heart we had both almost forgotten: you *will* let me have that until next time, won't you?

Then, too, there are so many others available. Couldn't we divide the burdens up a little? If we all carried them together no one person would feel the brunt of it. The others are allowed to go on playing: why must it be me who has to go home? The others are allowed to sample all of life's joys without harm or remorse: why should the bitterness of a bad con- science be my lot? The others go on dreaming in a soft twilight. They know not what they do, fortunate that they are. Why must you place me squarely within the sharp light of your countenance? Human beings do not fare well under such lighting. Or perhaps others do, but not I! Do you not have your special chosen souls who have been created and prepared just for this, those souls who have "a talent for religion"? For these it is a pleasure always to be by you. They know how it's done: they are experts in love. You'd be better off with them than with me. They will refuse you nothing of what you ask for. People in monasteries are there for just this. Priests are there for this. The Church is there for this. *Supplet Ecclesia.* Yes, a priest stands at the altar, all the way at the front, distracted and tired. Behind him in the nave he senses the absent-minded crowd with its dull confidence that "up there something's happening that somehow (we don't know exactly how) concerns us, too. Up there a man is at work and surely he knows what he's doing. He holds the office; he has the responsibility." But how is a man, even if he is a priest, to bear the burden of the whole community? He too is (fortunately) only a human being, only a sinner. At one time he had indeed attempted to give himself wholly, to hold nothing back. But everything has turned out very differently from what he had expected. The old man cannot be outsmarted all that easily, and when things are going well the old man, too, looks to tomorrow with hope. Still, the priest does know his theology. He knows that one man has atoned and suffered for all. He's the one who will do it. Even he, as priest, can put his burden over on that man's shoulder. "Come to me all you who are troubled and burdened." As priest, he has only to show men the path to this other man. His role is only an official one. He is but the channel, the middle-man. Grace works *ex operato*. And the work that is wrought is not his, but your work, O Lord, and it is on you that I deposit it. On you it remains to the end.

No one wants it. Everyone puts you off. It was under this sign that you appeared in the world. He came to what was his, but those who were his did not receive him. They know with precision that the King must be born in Israel. They also know the place—Bethlehem. They explain the way to all who ask about it, but they themselves fail to go there. And even in Bethlehem you are still too close for their taste. They throw you out of the country into exile. And in Nazareth they tolerate you only as long as you don't make yourself known. And the people cheer and applaud you only as long as you multiply their bread and tell them charming stories. And the disciples stand by you only as long as they continue to be blinded by the hope for an earthly kingdom and thus fail to hear you prophesy concerning the Cross. And then, on a wager, begins the "casting-out game." By rejecting your grace they begin casting you around to each other. You've become a ball and the way the game goes is that each player must get rid of the ball as quickly as possible. You become a burden especially to those closest to you: from the New Covenant, from your Church does the stone begin to roll. Mirroring that first man, all of us betray you. Mirroring the second man, whom you chose to be the Rock, all of us deny you. Mirroring all the others, we abandon you. And, driven out of your Church, you fall to the Jews, the people of yore. You fall into the enclosure of the covenant which you yourself had once erected around Israel. But here you are no less unwelcome. This covenant stood yesterday; tomorrow, when the Messiah comes, it will stand again. Today, however, we know no king but Caesar. And the ball rolls on, out of the covenant enclosure, and it chances over to the people outside—the nation of the heathen. For a moment it seems as though here you have won a place of your own. "I find no guilt in this man." But here, too, as always, you are found to be inopportune, for you trouble the political circles. The only convenient thing about you is that you can be shoved off on Herod, to become the pawn on the playing board of the powerful. And yet, as a wonder-worker you are found to be all too unproductive, so you roll back to the exit door, and now the earth's sensitive ground can really bear you no more. Out and up with him. Tormented and racked to death by those who know not what they do. Despised and slandered by those who could and should have known what they were doing. Betrayed and abandoned by those who could not but know what they did. Thus it is that you are totally expelled outside the farthest "outside," up like a Host over the earth which has rejected you, fastened onto the indifferent sky.

For even the Father no longer wants you. He loved the world so much that, for the sake of its salvation, he gave you up. He has abandoned you for the world, and now—I swear it!—he cannot use you. You must see for yourself how you will finish your struggle with the world—the world which has finished with you. The world is round and closed. You hang on the outside of the world and have no part in it. In this way are you its King. And all of us bend the knee and cry out: "Hail, King of the Jews!" And what we mean to say is: "Crucify him! Crucify him!" For you are wearisome to us all and an unbearable burden. Be off to do the work of deliverance for which you had volunteered. "Crucify him that we may be delivered from him! Crucify him that we may be delivered by him! Be off! *Tolle, crucifige!*"

CHAPTER VI

THE EYE OF THE PEACOCK

D O YOU HAVE ANY IDEA, Lord, of what you chose for yourself? Are you sure you understand the implications of your obedience? In nature's household, the poisonous residues and excretions of animals and men somehow dissolve: sweat evaporates, rain and rivers wash away the filth, corpses decay, and even the poisonous breath of our big cities is incapable of tarnishing the sky's purity. For the substances themselves are not impure; they only change their state. But in the household of the heart things are entirely different. There evil reigns, possessing no nature of itself since it is anti-natural, and it piles itself high like ever-growing refuse, and does not dissolve of itself and no worldly power (you know this, but men of course don't) is able to sweep it away. In the north of France you can see factories, and next to them black mountains of slag tower ten times higher than the city's rooftops. These sinister hills that exhale a dark curse attempt in vain to form a bit of landscape. And you want to demolish the towers and mountains of sin? You want to drink up this ocean of infallibly lethal poisons? You want to transform your sublime Heart into a purification plant for the world?

How will you be able to bear the contact of even a single sin, you who are wholly pure? Watch out! You will surely be deeply shocked when one of us casually brushes by you in the street. You will look into this person's soul and, in the depths of it, behold the mass of entangled worms that dwells there. You will even look back and see all the petty and cowardly malice which has accumulated there over the years. And I tell you: already you will feel a rising nausea. But it is not enough merely to graze this sinner, to bear contact with him for just one moment, to feel his putrid breath upon your face. You must try to take his sins into yourself, to declare yourself one with them; not only to study them from without, but to taste all their reality and malice from within. You will have to imagine that they are not the sins of this wholly alien person—sins which basically have nothing to do with you—but your very own. Now they belong to you, and it is quite beside the point whether you committed them or not. I cannot list for you all of the palpable and evident things which can hide in a soul, things of which it is fully conscious and which from time to time even weigh it down a bit: all the half-conscious and long-forgotten things (for man cannot bear his shame for long and likes to forget it quickly), finally all of the unconscious things that can hide in a soul. I cannot enumerate all of the possible sins man would be able to commit, sins for the realization of which all that is missing from the human side is the exterior impulse, the opportunity, the right social relations, the temptation, or a bad environment. I cannot describe all of this to you in detail. We men are not in the least aware of the proportions and impact of our guilt. Or we weigh our guilt by false standards: the small things that we wholly overlook can be a heavy burden on the scales of eternity. Thus, man mostly thinks only of the evil deeds he has committed, and the evil thoughts he has fostered appear to him unimportant because no one sees them. But you will encounter something else which man does not himself see: the void. The lack of love. The incalculable and irreparable deficit of that goodness which God had intended for him. The gaping hollow which man no longer notices because he himself is hollow. But you, who are the fullness of love and action, will cry out into this void and will grow stiff in this winter of love. It is not the greatest sins which will be most painful to you. These are well-rounded and easily recognized, and with one brave jolt you can swallow them down like a toad. But what will you in your greatness do with the vermin? For sin is mostly small. It is petty, lacking both greatness and dignity. Sin is pettiness itself, repulsive and greasy. You know what I mean: this sort of spiritual bartering and endless calculation. How far can I go and still not have to confess it? What further concession can I make to my lust? Where is the borderline between mortal and venial sin? (The latter I'll take on myself!) These trade agreements with God! That's the way things mostly are with us. What's your opinion of this our lovely attitude, O Son of Love? Once you brandished a braided cord and whipped these shopkeeper-souls out of your Father's temple. Now you are the one who is fettered and all of them approach you in order to spit their repugnant filth down your throat. Be careful not to disdain or overlook any one of these "small" sins. You must savor each of them separately, because otherwise your work would not be complete. Even the course of one single day in the life of one person is an uninterrupted chain of small betrayals, of innocent jabs against love. Oh your work is great! But there are many of them: your Father has made them count-less as the sand of the sea—millions, billions—and they will descend upon you like swarms of locusts and not one green leaf will remain on you.

You have taken it upon yourself to bear their dis-grace. And, indeed, every person must bear it. But they themselves don't do it. They know well enough how to do what is disgraceful, but they think that the shame of their deeds vanishes without trace and is lost in time's oblivion. They know nothing about the Book of Life and eternity's memory. They shake off their shame and go on their way, relieved. But this millennial shame rains down on you, an endless tor-rent. The leprosy of millions covers you, and you go down into a nameless sewer. What is, then, the mean-ing of shame? To stand in the pillory is a small thing, for in the end all the ones below looking up at the shackled man are themselves sinners, and perhaps one or another of them already realizes this. To have to strip naked in the midst of an elegant *soirée* is a small thing, for, after all, everyone present has a body under his clothes. To have to proclaim one's innermost vices before all the world is a small thing, since any daily newspaper acquaints us with all of men's possible crimes. But shame itself, shame-in-itself, that shame which none of us wants to taste or has ever tasted: what is it? You will find out. You will be shamed before all the world, before the dead stones of the Mount of Olives, before every creature, and, most of all, before your Father. You would like to descend to all depths of the abyss, to crawl into every hole: but you are yourself the abyss and the hole. And don't think that no one notices you. We all have our eye on you; in you all of us see our shame, and in you we despise our shame.

You cannot be rid of the disgust you feel. For now you are disgust itself. Everything base has entered you, and you are an aversion not only to yourself, but to all of us. We are the society of decent men, and you stand outside. We can excuse each other's peccadilloes and again raise our hat as we cross in the street. But before you we can only turn away with contempt. We form a community, a closed ring, and the very thought that a being like you would belong to our circle is unbearable.

Is fear finally coming over you—a fear men know nothing about? I don't mean fear of some impending, some definite catastrophe. For such fear is limited: it has its object and man's consciousness is directed to that object. And, with us men, hope always remains as an inseparable companion of fear. Maybe I can still escape from the burning house; perhaps we can still succeed in reaching the caved-in-mine-shaft in time; perhaps I will still be pardoned even at the last minute? What you suffer is a shapeless fear. It is a sea of fear without shores, fear-in-itself. The fear which is the core of sin. The fear of God and his inescapable judgment. The fear of hell. The fear of never again seeing the face of the Father for all eternity. The fear that love itself and every creature with it have dropped you irretrievably into the abyss. You fall into the bottomless; you are lost. Not the faintest shimmer of hope delimits this fear. For in what could you still have hope? That the Father might still pardon you? He will not, cannot, does not want to do it. Only for the price of your sacrifice does he intend to pardon the world: the world, not you. Nothing at all is said about anything beyond your fear. Mercy? But you are yourself God's mercy, and it consists in your own ruination. Someone has to be the scapegoat, and you are it. Indeed, you yourself wanted it this way. Do you want to avert God's lightning-bolt from men? Then it will have to strike you.

"Father," you cry out, "if it is possible . . . " But now it is not even possible. Every fragment and shred of possibility has disappeared. You cry into the void: "Father!" And the echo resounds. The Father has

109

heard nothing. You have sunk too low into the depths: how are those up in heaven still to hear you? "Father, I am your Son, your beloved Son, born from you before time began!" But the Father no longer knows you. You have been eaten up by the leprosy of all creation: how should he still recognize your face? The Father has gone over to your enemies. Together they have plotted their war-plan against you. He has loved your murderers so much that he has betrayed you, his Only-begotten. He has given you up like a lost outpost; he has let go of you like a lost son. Are you sure that he still really exists? Is there a God? If a God existed he would be love itself; he certainly could not be sheer hardness, more unrelenting than a wall of bronze. If there were a God, he would have to manifest himself at least in his majesty; you would have to feel at least a breath of his eternity; you would at least be allowed to kiss the hem of his garment when, in his sublimeness, he walked away over you, perhaps crushing you heedlessly underfoot. Oh, how gladly you would allow yourself to be trampled by that adored foot! But, instead of gazing into the pupil of God's eye, you stare into the void of a black eye-socket. And so you stagger over to men; now that eternal love is dead and the chill of the world's expanse wraps you in its ice, you seek some measure of life in men's animal warmth. But these are asleep. Let them sleep; let even the beloved disciple sleep. They would never understand that God no longer loves.

And then, like a ray of light, the thought flashes through your soul: what does it matter if he lets me fall if only, in exchange, he loves mankind? If I am to be the ransom money, then eternal darkness is not too great a price for the eternal light—MY eternal light!—which they are now to inherit in my place. Father, your will be done in them as also in me. Your loving will in them, your wrathful will in me . . . But the comforting angel abandons you again and Satan approaches you from the left. He shows you the world, mankind after redemption. Can you possibly bear the sight? Do you understand what you see before you? I will tell you very simply what the point is: your work is done in vain. Before the birth of Christ, after the birth of Christ: by and large everything remains the same. We had expected a torrent of grace; we thought that God would pour forth his Spirit according to his promise and that a holy kingdom would arise in the last days. Yet nothing at all is going to change. A few of your disciples will tell about your existence; people will listen for a moment, amazed by this new tale; and, for a while, it will seem as though your Church possessed a new spiritual vitality, a power from above to transform the world. But soon this world will begin to rub off its color on the Church: she herself will paint her cheeks with the changing colors of the world, and soon she will be asked what exactly is the newness she has brought. And this question will be justified. She will be asked for her identification papers: not for proofs in books and not for proofs of the legitimacy of her mission, rather for proofs of her power. She will herself be entangled in the general sinning, and the sins of Christians will be found to weigh more than the sins of Jews and pagans. Therefore her voice will strain and, stammering, she will emit as best she can demented and useless discourses full of unction. And she will be persecuted because she has deceived the world with hypocritical promises—and this persecution, too, will be justified. The deceit, however, will revert to you who founded her and sent her forth. You will be guilty of the fact that men have lost their childlike faith in the gods and now, despairing with disillusionment in you, they pass over to a resolute godlessness. Do you see what you have caused with your redemption? You wanted to restore to the blind the light of their eyes, but now those who gained back their sight are doubly guilty. When they crucified you in the first instance they did not know what they were doing; their sin resembled the native cruelty of a beast of prey: it was in their nature. But now they know what they do. You have drawn back the veil from the mystery of eternal love. You have placed them directly before God's threefold abyss as initiates into the divine economy. Now their sin becomes a revolt against love. What used to be pardonable and excusable has, through you, become deadly and unforgivable. At one time they used to shoot children's play-arrows up to heaven; but now you have placed in their hands the sharp, poisoned arrow with which they can strike at the bull's-eye of God's Heart. You miscalculated. You believed you were bringing redemption, whereas in reality you have multiplied sin tenfold. In a hundred different ways they will find in you an occasion for sin. With your doctrine you will be a vexation to them, and they will take offense at each of your statements—rightly so, as you will have to admit, for what you say can be misunderstood and is dangerous for the masses. Every error, every imbecility will be referred to you and will be clothed with your words. Like Furies they will tear your Gospel apart and wave the bloody tatters against each other. And those who are loyal to you will further sin against your redemption: for God's love has now become cheap and for small coins of remorse an absolution can be gotten at the confessional automat. Do you understand what you have done. You have made sin too easy for them. Your redemption is a derision: it redeems men *to* sin! We must avoid you, make a wide detour around you, for you are a seducer of mankind. You are a peril to all who encounter you. You are a contagious disease. Believe me, men would do better to keep to their nature and their instincts. The only thing you have accomplished is to give men a bad conscience.

No, they really are right if they reject you. They do not want an offer which leads to such losses. What they need is bread and love—the love which they already know and which you do not know, being a virgin: more than this they cannot grasp. Your religion is not for the masses. Your priests will proclaim your demands from their pulpits, but no one will heed them and many will be amazed at how alien you are to the world. You will twist around the heads and consciences of very many so that they no longer know the true order of things.

But I must admit I still see your chosen ones there, your particular friends, the "apples of your eyes": your holy ones. I will not now subject them to close scrutiny, adding up the many years during which they fought against your love hand and foot, until you finally razed the fortress of their soul to the ground with violence. And what do you give them instead? Your Cross, your road to Calvary. The Father abandoned you, and now you, in turn, abandon them. Your love is cruel. What kind of redemption is this? Could you not yourself carry the cross once and for all? Are you so weak that another has to come after you to help you carry it? A boasting Atlas, you volunteered to bear the burden of the world on your shoulders. You overestimated your strength: on that short road you collapse three times, and Simon has to carry your beam. Can't you leave those you call your own finally in peace? You deliver them to the wild beasts; you let them burn like living torches; in concentration camps they are slowly and diabolically tortured to death. And even this is not enough. You turn them over to all possible demons; you pull them down to share your pit of fear and revulsion, and, as your Apostle says, you let them become the refuse and offscouring of the world and the laughing-stock of creation. In their body they are to complete for you what is still lacking to your sufferings, what you did not know how to suffer to its full term.

Certainly, in order to suffer a great and strong heart is required. But your Heart became so small and weak and wholly impotent that you yourself would not recognize it. To suffer one ought to know how to love. But you no longer love: your love, which once pealed solemnly like a massive bell, now clatters as pitiably as a rattle on Good Friday. It would be too easy to suffer if one could still love. Love has been taken from you. The only thing you still feel is the burning void, the hollow which it has left behind. It would be a joy for you if, from the depths of hell, you could still, and for all eternity, love the Father who rejected you. But love has been taken from you. You wanted to give everything away, didn't you? It requires no great skill to give everything up so long as one can still keep love. It only gets serious when love gives itself up. Love was your Heart's heart, your soul's bread, the eternal breath of your person. You lived on love; you had no other thought but love; you were love. Now it has been taken away: you are smothering, starving; you are a stranger to yourself. You are dying the true *Liebestad*, the true love-death, for we hear love's death-rattle and witness its last contortions.

All of this must be so. And it must be hidden, and men have no inkling of what is occurring. They simply walk on past it as over the dark pipes and drains that form the gruesome catacombs under our big cities. Up above the sun is beaming; peacocks fan out their tails; young people frolic with glee, their light clothes puffed by the wind—and no one knows the price.

CHAPTER VII

THE INTRUDER

I F YOU HAVE FIRE IN THE HOUSE, guard it well in a fire-proof hearth. Cover it up, for if only one spark escapes and you fail to see it, you and everything that is yours will fall prey to the flames. If you have the Lord of the World in you, in your fireproof heart, fence him in well, be careful as you carry him about, lest he begin to make demands and you no longer know whither he pushes you. Hold the reins tightly in your hand. Don't let go of the rudder. God is dangerous. God is a consuming fire. God intended this for you. Take heed of his words: "Whoever sets his hand to the plough and looks back, is not worthy of me. Whoever does not love me more than father and mother, more than beloved and country, more than even himself, is not worthy of me." Watch out: he is a good dissembler. He begins with a small love, a small flame, and before you realize it he has gotten total hold of you and you are caught. If you let yourself be caught you are lost, for heavenwards there are no limits. He is God—accustomed to infinity. He sucks you upwards like a cyclone, whirls you up and away like a waterspout.

Look out: man is made for measure and limits, and only in the finite does he find rest and happiness. But this God knows nothing of measure. He is a seducer of hearts.

Do you see him standing there on the steps of the Temple amid the seething crowd? Do you see him stretching out his arms and raising that voice of his, which alone suffices to make a human heart quake to its very foundations? "Let whoever thirsts come to me and let whoever believes in me drink from me! For Scripture says: 'Streams of living water flow out from him'." Stay away from this drink. For he did indeed say to that woman: "Whoever drinks earthly water will again be thirsty; but whoever drinks of the water I give him will never thirst again for all eternity." Watch out, for it is also written: "Whoever drinks of wisdom will again, and more than ever, thirst." I fear that such a person will only then experience what thirst is, and, the more voraciously he begins to drink, the more unbearably will his suffering increase. Drawn into the law of the boundless, he will fall victim to vertigo. Take care: he invites you to lose your soul in order to gain it back. He means love. He demands the impossible from man. He doesn't realize that men are made for a happiness within bounds: a few years of companionship with someone more loved than the rest, a walk through the fields, or simply a bowl of strawberries. A painting, a book, a bench in the shade. A cozy fire. A stroll in the biting night. The flush of battle. The majesty of death. Always an eternal meaning, but contained within the precise contour of a moment. That is sufficient and ineffable. Here the world ripens and rounds itself out like a fruit and laden with such divine meaning it falls before the feet of the Eternal. Ask the poets . . .

But for our interests he is a danger. It was not wise of him to reveal himself so candidly, for his words sound like open revolt: "I have come to cast down fire upon the earth, and what do I desire but that it should blaze high?" If he were to keep his soul's extravagance to himself, or if, for that matter, he were to make redemption flare high one glorious time before the ecstatic eyes of spectators in the performance of a fireworks of love, no one would have any objections. We could then indulge our applause, "insistent, roaring applause," as the critics say, in gratitude for this unexpected and solemn occasion which has thus (and wholly free of charge!) come to enrich creation. We would then justly be proud that the circus of the human heart, already so rich in extraordinary acrobats, should find its crowning climax in God's *salto mortale*. But he does not let matters rest there. He sets his death-jump up as a model; he lures men from their limits out into the same inevitably deadly adventure. His fire is to burn on in others. Now and then he actually succeeds, like dynamite, in blasting a soul into the air, and far and wide the windows rattle and the foundations of houses quake.

What does one do when there is threat of a conflagration? One hedges it in. One attempts to deprive the fire of its fuel and, if necessary, whole city-blocks have to be blown up and demolished. A bare strip is made through the burning forest, or, if it is the plains burning, a wide ditch is dug. So, too, must we attempt to hem him in. Create all around him a space void of air where neither fire nor love can breathe! Choke him—but gently.

Take him at his word and things will be easiest: "My kingdom is not of this world." Here you have the key. His kingdom is not of this world, is not this world. How sublime! How heavenly! He possesses a higher kingdom. Praise him, boost him up into this higher kingdom! Let him have his kingdom and then he'll have to let us have ours. You needn't show him the door with boorish ill-manners. You must do it elegantly: You can honor him out of your house; in the best and least suspicious sense you can drive him out with compliments. Do not dispute him anything, rather make all the concessions: that he originates from above and we from below, that he is the light of the world and the darkness has not grasped it, that he has come in order to return again to the Father. For you must understand: he desires nearness; he would like to live in you and commingle his breath with your breathing. He would like to be with you until the end of the world. He knocks at all the souls. He makes himself small and inconspicuous so as to be able to partake of all their little transactions and concerns. He approaches quietly so as not to disturb or be recognized; he comes to be present incognito in the full hubbub of the earth's annual fair. He seeks trust, intimacy; he is a beggar for your love. Here is where you must really stand firm so that the boundaries won't be blurred. He is God and he must remain such. He ought not demean himself. It is a God-fearing thing to remind him of what he owes to himself. When he suddenly jumps out of his ambush and grips at your heart with one of his famous handholds, and your heart goes wild with throbbing, then you must quickly cast yourselves down and say with all humility: "Lord, go away from me. I am a sinful man!" That's an obvious distance, you see. And when he looks at you sorrowfully and silently attempts to make his solitude visible to you, remain strong. Do him homage and say: "I am not worthy that you should come under my roof" (but leave the rest out!). Or when you invite him to come to your house, keep your composure. Do not by any means abandon yourselves and, abolishing distances, start washing his feet like some prostitute, or give him a kiss, or anoint his head with oil. If he should sit in the last place, say to him: "Friend, come forward!" and force him to sit in the first place. Adore him as when he was transfigured up on the mountain. With his devotees, build three huts there for him. And see to it that he does not come down again.

All of this is easier than you think. It is through and through a religious mode of thought, and what does God desire from you if not religion? The recognition of the "infinite qualitative difference" between God and the world. Whether you understand this in a more dialectical or a more liberal sense is wholly up to you.

In one's public life it isn't at all difficult. Here we have only to adhere strictly to the line of demarcation once it has been drawn. His kingdom is not of this world. For this reason he has no business in our worldly affairs. Let him have his cathedrals and he'll let us have our banks, our shops, our politics, our schools, the works of our culture, our country. Let him have his game preserve, the "national park" of his churches. We pledge neither to fell timber nor to hunt there. Our roads will be built to curve around this protective zone, and within this area he will be allowed to raise his strange mountain animals and his amazingly gnarled, dwarf stone-pines within reach of the glaciers. Imagine that perchance one of our researchers—say, a philosopher of religion—should mistakenly wander into his garden. He gathers up a few samples of the rare little plants that are found there at every step and then brings them home to classify them according to the most recent findings of psychology. Surely he will not hold this attempt at some contact against us. But let us otherwise have not a single word from him! In your affairs of state see to it that you proceed according to the immanent laws of reason, of philanthropy, of the general welfare and of a healthy instinct for self-preservation. Although altruistic love of neighbor may indeed have a certain justification in the domain of private morality, the state as a whole and the nation must be erected upon the solid foundation of collective self-interest—that is, if state and nation are not to collapse immediately as unrealistic utopias. Let us, therefore, have no word from him in our councils, no word from him in the front pages of our papers, no word from him in our peace conferences. The world is the world's. It would be advisable to restrict the clergy to the realm of the Church and not to grant them any rights or power whatsoever in public matters. You will thus be doing *them* a service, since politics has always spoiled the Church and jeopardized her influence. It would be wise to establish a sharp separation of secular subjects and religion in the schools. Once "religious instruction" becomes a carefully isolated subject, on the margin of twenty others, then the danger of religion encroaching on other concerns is no longer very great. The student will realize on his own that what is here involved is a kind of elective without practical significance, and which in any event is of no consequence for the final grade. With this you will have the youth on your side. In critical times, however, it cannot hurt to direct those with intense religious needs to the sacral agencies set up for this purpose on the busier streets where everyone can freshen up practically free of charge. In this way, religious needs will not escalate to the point of a dangerous unrest. This policy is part of the public hygiene, and in any case it saves you the trouble of having to muck through the turbid waters of the religious problem. In all of this your watchword will be: "Immunity against the religious bacteria!" The institutions of the church will be there as innoculation and antidote. Then you will have order.

In cultural life we must press for clarity. A religious bookstore should be recognizable from far-off and in other bookstores, totally accessible to everyone, you must take care that no religious writings lie about openly. In art you must see to it that religious objects are designated as such so far as possible, and no secular work of art ought to include an ambiguous "religious atmosphere." Religious artists would do well to form a special guild. We are to foster, as much as we are able, Christian educational establishments which show a tendency to present confessional peculiarities as constituting a separate culture in itself, for in this way the rest of the atmosphere is purified. The separation of philosophy and theology, of the natural order and Christian faith, of sinful world and redemptive realm, of mankind and the Cross, must be portrayed to both sides as being a significant achievement of modern times, indeed as the decisive safeguard for each. Associations which must perforce disregard these laws of the public weal are to be forbidden as dangerous to the state. On the other hand, we are to foster those groups which consider Christianity too holy for the street, too pure for this world, and which consequently confine religion to those "hallowed halls" which as pious relics from the Middle Ages, under state protection, enhance the beauty of our cities' streets. (Support tourism!)

But all of this is not enough. He still seems to have the inner kingdom of souls to himself. After being driven out of public life, he can continue to wield his seductive power in the private sphere of conscience. You must double your watchfulness! On this point each one must be warned individually. As a simple rule of thumb you can take the practice of the overwhelming majority of Christians: their instinct has obviously chosen the right course. They have found the golden mean between life's immediate demands and those other totalitarian claims. For your daily life, erect a chapel somewhere in a snug corner. Set up an altar there, with a kneeler in front of it. There he'll be preserved; aside from your ceremonious attendance at Sunday Mass, you'll be able to visit him daily there for a few moments. "My five minutes a day." For you that will be your soul's wholesome morning exercise; for him it will be a sign that you have not forgotten to include him in your thoughts. You can ask him to bless the day's tasks, and in this way a kind of bridge will have been built. Beyond this, you can even formulate a so-called "good intention": by which you promise to fulfill your day's work "for his honor." Then away you go, and don't forget to take the key to the sanctuary from its lock and to guard it well! Seriously now, see to it that he in no way succeeds in encroaching upon your private affairs. Do not be troubled by anyone who comes with Bible quotes and pious sayings to prove to you that you ought to pray always and always to cultivate your familiarity with him. No: this would only disturb

125

your work, which beyond all doubt is willed by both God and nature. Tell him that you are heartily thankful if in the meantime he busies himself with your redemption, remits your sins, provides the necessary graces, and that it will be a pleasure for you to accept the results of his efforts once it is all over. There is still time before then, and you can be of no help to him.

But still we have not won on all fronts. The separation of prayer and daily life is only a beginning. The time of prayer remains when you stand before him eye to eye, the time of voluntary or involuntary examination of conscience, the time when his unfathomable eye once again pierces you and the subdued fire could break out anew, the time when you are shaken by inner anguish over yourself and an inner longing for purity and wholeness and the tears are not far . . . These are dangerous moments: the time of enticement to love. Remain strong! Don't be an old woman! Repeat to yourself constantly that nothing lasting can be built on soft feelings. These melting aspirations are not in keeping with your character. And have you not time and again experienced the fact that these moods blow away, leaving less trace than wind-driven clouds, and that afterwards all is exactly the same as before? Do not base your religion on such unclear and blurred things. Perhaps this sentimental side does really exist in him; but for you it must suffice to indulge sentiment by putting a little holy picture in your prayer-book. And if you still can't be rid of his gaze, then pray until you no longer see him. This can be done! You can pray God away from you!

You can pray the nearby God away to a distant God. You can pray so ardently that you are totally consumed by your own words and have no time or possibility left to listen to God's voice. You overwhelm him with requests until he has to keep his silent. Since you, of course, need a thousand things from him, he will never be able to arrive at making his demand known. By fulfilling these religious obligations—or, what is still nobler, by voluntary exercises of piety—you have spared yourself having to listen to the troublesome voice. Believe me, this method is by far the best, and if you remain faithful to it, sooner or later you will succeed in putting your own religion in the place of his. Then you'll finally have peace. But everything must happen in the name of piety and Christianity. The essential thing is that you are protected against him. Tell him that he is God, that consequently he knows everything. Then you'll not have to go over every single detail with him. Or tell him that you are, after all, only human: this will touch him and move him to compassion. Or tell him that you have boundless trust in his grace and that you believe—sure as he's savior!—that everything will be well in the end. This will stir his honor as redeemer and disarm him. Show him a naive, child-like devotion, unswerving and unalloyed. Look up at him with demure and innocent eyes (the "creature's pure glance") and he will not dare to initiate you into his confusing mysteries. Let not his kingdom be of your world. Let him keep his darkness, your light has no need to grasp it.

There still remains the Church herself, his place of refuge: the Church and the churches. Here is where he has gathered himself up, here where he has mustered all the armies of his grace. Here is where he must be definitively defeated. Then there will be no more remaining for him; then he will have lost the ground under his feet; then will his kingdom, in all truth, not be among us. But take comfort: this battle, too, is already almost won. Everything hinges on the imperative of also isolating him within the Church. For here too (and here above all) is where he would most like to relate to human beings in a human way. This is where he has invented the miracle of his Eucharist: he is in you and you are in him—a wedding-feast without end between you and him, compared with which the union of man and wife is but a brief and poor effort. In this garment of bread and wine he desires to dwell among us with his bodily presence, sharing in men's joys and sorrows. But you must remind him of the awesome distance between you, of the Eucharist's symbolic sense! Teach him how to think along more eschatological lines! Ultimately, we are in time and he in eternity. And to make sure he understands what you mean, throw him out tabernacle and all! We want to think of him in a more spiritual and sublime manner! Let his presence be spiritual, and spiritual his kingdom! As for all these human, these all-too-human accretions—these statues, confessionals, kneelers, Ways of the Cross, paintings and clouds of incense: away with all such scandal of proximity! Let the atmosphere be clear between God and you! Away with this ambiguous medium, this half-human, half-divine mediation, this twilight of the senses! Has he not risen and does he not sit at the Father's right hand? And will he not come soon enough to judge the living and the dead? Let us be sober, and when we go to the Eucharist let us not forget to take our best hat along with our hymnal.

You can also hide him behind the iconostasis. Back there, unseen by the profane crowd, the bearded priests perform their duties, and only at a distance can one hear the echoes of chants and bells jingling. The mystery is thrice holy, an image and reenactment of the heavenly divine liturgy, and any direct contact with it would constitute a profanation. For the people the saints on the icon-screen must suffice, bigger than life, bodiless, inimitable images whose garments are heavily weighed down with hieratic folds as they raise towards us earnest, rejecting hands. To these may you pray, begging for their intercession; Tabor's sublime light, in which the Lord is enthroned, would surely blind you. Only the very few are considered worthy to approach him ecstatically, after they have purified themselves on Mount Athos for long decades. It is indeed rewarding to be passionate about the beauty of icons, for with the spiritual realm that this beauty reveals we have been freed from the intrusion of his love!

And you, good Catholic, have named him the

"prisoner of the tabernacle." There you hold him in tight custody, within the darkness of the golden chest. The key to it is somewhere in a drawer in the sacristy. So there he sits, and can consider himself lucky if during the day a few old people come and pray a rosary before him. "Have you any notion of desolate aloneness?" The people outside rush about their affairs; with briefcases in their hands, or book-bags, or shopping baskets they hurry by the church, which is a dead facade interrupting the row of colorful display windows. None of them thinks of him. For now no one needs him. Typewriters rattle away, factories give off their smoke, schoolchildren solve their math problems, housewives go through their piles of wash: everything follows its course, a closed and smooth cycle that has nothing to do with him and in which no provision at all is made for him. Somewhere, at a late Mass, a little bell rings at the consecration: for whom? And then the sacristan cleans up, covers the altar, and dead quiet reigns around the one who has been pronounced dead.

The tabernacle has its advantage. One knows where he resides. And, consequently, one also knows where he is not (though it is easier to dispose of God's more general "all-seeing eye"). In his corner he quietly toils away at the work of redemption. And once in a year, or perhaps even twelve times a year, one does him the favor of letting him realize his work of love in one's person. One "practices" (laurels to the inventor of this word!). Or, rather, we allow him to practice on us.

Often he has tried to break out of his prison. Once he let it be known that he would like a feast in honor of the Eucharist. And so we then took him out and led him once a year through streets and fields. Spectators stood about startled and silently lifted their hats. Then again he let us see his Heart, wreathed in thorns, surmounted by a cross, and a great flame which he could no longer hold back shoots up from it. Again we set a feast. We consecrate our houses to him, and all over he beams forth from colorful lithographs. All of this is an affront to good taste. One doesn't say it out loud, but at least educated people agree on one thing: the whole thing has a considerable dose of *kitsch*. It would be much better to leave all of this in the dark; in this way it would at least not be profaned, even if it would be forgotten. As soon as it comes into the limelight a coat of saccharine insipidness settles upon it like mildew. Pomaded locks curl down over the shoulders, and the pained turn of the eyes makes you slightly nauseous.

No, it would be much better if in the future he renounces all such attempts to escape. Let him be satisfied with his redeemer's lot. We are indeed happy that he chose this profession. But let him only see to it that he sets up his workshop outside our city gates.

He stands at the street corners and offers his Heart for the taking. For it is written that Wisdom went out into the town squares and offered herself as a great banquet—to no avail. They all rush by. There's no demand for him. He miscalculated. When things get serious, an offer of love is straightaway turned down

131

by man, who otherwise cannot boast loudly enough of his need for love. He extricates himself from love's arms. The most interior of voices warns him: "Have nothing to do with him, the danger is too great. Tell him you're sorry. Tell him that you've bought a farm, rented a yoke of oxen for the day, that you've taken a wife who'll do for the time being. Tell him you're really sorry. The birds have their nests and the foxes their lairs, but the Son of Man—and this is why you're most sincerely sorry—has nothing: no friend, no human heart upon which to rest his divine Head."

CHAPTER VIII

JAILHOUSE AND COCOON

Y OU ARE IN PRISON and I am in prison. I know,
Lord, that you are in your prison for my sake and
that you remain in yours only because I remain in
mine. Both of them belong together; both are one and
the same dungeon. If you could succeed in freeing me
from my confinement, you too would be free. The dividing wall between us would topple and we would
both enjoy the same freedom. I, too, could perhaps free
you by freeing myself, and in this case as well we
would both be freed. But that's just it! This is precisely
what you can't do and what I myself can't do.

I know your secret; you want to share my destiny.
But I am deeply buried within myself and I cannot
burst open the gates to this hell. You thought it
would be easier for two, and you offered to help me.
You buried yourself in my cave. But, because my solitude is lonely, yours also became lonely. And now
we wait one for the other, separated by this wall. I
well know that the fault lies with me, and not at all
with you. You have done everything that was possible. You have suffered, made atonement in my place,

paid for everything in advance down to the last drop.
But there is one thing you can't do, and this is something I can't do either. I should . . . but I cannot. I
should want to, but I don't. I wish I could want to,
but I don't want to want to. How do things stand
then? How can this be? I don't understand it. They
say you blotted out sin and made atonement for it.
They say you effaced sin, not just covered it over, and
that henceforth it no longer exists in the eyes of God.
And yet sin is precisely this: that I do not want what
God wants. And I can't see how this opposition
on my part could be broken. I can't see how this
prison wall which holds me captive could be pierced
through.

Do you know what I mean, Lord? It isn't easy to
explain this to you. For I myself don't know exactly
how it occurs, how all of this fits together. When I
reflect upon it, it's like knotted briars and my soul
gets trapped in them. My soul is like the young lamb
that wandered off among the thorns. I'll try to tell
you how it happened.

At first everything is simple. I see that I cannot do
what I would like to do. Too, I know precisely what I
ought to do. You've often told me yourself, the priest
has often told me, I have told myself. This, then, is
not what's lacking. The will is lacking: the being able
to want. There is a will in me that wants, and there is
another will in me (the same one!) that does not want.
"What I do is incomprehensible to me, for I do not do
what I want—the good—but I accomplish what I

abhor—the evil. Willing the good matters to me, but not accomplishing it. Precisely what I want, I do not do—the good—but I do what I do not want—the evil. The interior man indeed takes joy in God's law, but I am aware of another law in my members that wars against the law of my spirit and holds me imprisoned under the law of sin which reigns in my members. Unhappy man that I am! Who will redeem me from this death-bearing body?" Thus it is that I am rent apart in my innermost will, and the same thing in me that wants is precisely what does not want. And this is why I cry out to you from the depths of my Prison of Unwilling: Make me want!

But ought one to pray thus? To be sure, you can give everything: every relief, every grace. But I myself must want and take the decisive step. I lie upon my bed of pleasure and this pleasure disgusts me, and I would like to break loose and stand up. And the only thing lacking is the decision, the action that really effects it. Can I say to the friend who stands near me and wants to help me: "Give me the decision"? He can point out reasons; give me food to strengthen me, reach out his hand. But how should he be able to provide me with the indivisible atom of freedom, that flash of real willing? From nowhere except myself can this deed come to birth. But I do not want to. For I love my pleasure; this bitterness is sweet to me, and I cannot make up my mind to renounce it. And if I should force myself to do this externally and put myself in fetters externally, my soul would not for all that have turned away from bitter pleasure-seeking. If I went without sinning for awhile, it was only because my soul lacked convenient opportunities.

Often it seems indecent for me to be incessantly accosting you with requests that are not seriously meant. While one of my folded hands entreats you: "Deliver me from evil!", the other one is moaning: "Spare me and let me yet have the evil I love!" Request on request ascends to you and none of them is solid and true. While I speak, another voice speaks right along, like a demonic echo: "Your Kingdom come—my kingdom come." "Your will be done—my will be done." "Give me your daily bread—let me have my daily bread." If I were a saint, then my voice would perhaps grow silent and I could love you with my whole heart and fulfill your law with a perfect will. But I am one of the half-and-halves, and just as my will is only one-half, so too my prayer. Therefore, I greatly fear you cannot fulfill it, and that you will turn away from me just as you spew out the lukewarm.

And now I come to what is even worse, and here the tangle becomes impossible. If I can't do the whole thing at once, I should at least be able to do it little by little. You would like to see me make progress, slowly gaining my strength back and returning to health. The small steps I have made could, in place of a sudden change, bring me gradually closer to the goal. But this is not what's happening. It seems to me that the opposite is rather the case. When I was young and my body was developing, I believed in progress in the spirit. A dream of Paradise haunted me, and I am not sure whether as a past or a future reality. An image hovered before me, enticing and spell-binding. How I was to reach it I did not know. This was not important to me, for I believed that all my ways led towards it, even the crooked ones, and unexpectedly it could be reached some distant day. It was a mirage in the desert. Gradually the pace of life began to stagnate and become a walking in place. The beautiful image over me faded and blurred. It transformed itself into a star and an ideal whose unreachableness constitutes a part of its beauty—like a sunken city which on calm days can be seen under the skiff. But slime and algae constantly settle on it like a veil, and soon all we'll be able to make out will be a few dark, shapeless masses. Everything was thriving as luxuriantly as Sleeping Beauty's castle. I began to look at my ideal as one of those ruses of life which make hopelessness more bearable for the unsalvageably mediocre person. From that time on, despair barely conceded began to descend upon my heart. I understood that I would never reach it. I weighed myself and found myself too light. I measured how deeply sin had struck its roots in me and I saw clearly that I would never succeed in uprooting it. I would have needed a native generosity, energy, and excellence of spirit which I did not possess. Not one of my thoughts or deeds was free of the scurf of my pettiness, of my shopkeeper's soul. To me nothing was so irrefutable as my essential small-mindedness, which compelled me to set up limits everywhere.

With these limits I stumbled on you, the unconditional one, and here everything now became dreadful.
I felt your infiniteness; I knew you could not forbear
provoking me to total self-surrender, to the leap into
your glorious light. But as your adversary there
stood, bright as day, the inadequacy of my nature.
The more your grace tried to remove my burden, to
carry me in its arms across the river, the heavier and
stiffer I made myself. I knew you could not succeed.
You could, to be sure, forgive my sin over and over
again; for a brief moment you could hold me high in
the pure reaches of the sun. But my gravity strained
inexorably downwards again. Thus it was that the
prison grew up all around me. Externally I put on an
appearance of careless mirth and experienced resignation; within, however, in the deep cavern of despair,
there swarms a putrid rabble that hates the light;
wasted opportunities, rejected graces, invincible de-
jection—the smell of putrifaction. Things went so
far that the merest glimmer of a new challenge from
you sufficed to elicit the crass No of my unwilling.
Better to call it quits altogether than to continue on
this disgraceful blunderer's course. And if you were
to try to burst my prison door open from the outside,
from the inside I would resist you with clairvoyant
despair. The mask and my face have inter-grown. I
was a Christian: I believed it all, did like the others;
but I was no longer redeemable. Or, if I still was, then
only in the pitiful sense that I was awaiting in the
distant beyond the fire which consumes prisons that

in this world are definitive and which releases stiff limbs from their armor. I came to regret the fact of ever having met you.

I was entangled in lies. When I said to myself "I can," "I will," a hundred experiences had taught me that it was not so. The clay does not suffice for the statue you intended to form with me. But when I said to myself "I cannot," "I will not," this was a sin, for I gave you the lie. I held two yardsticks in my hand, both of them correct, both of them well-gauged; but they contradicted each other. And I often thought that pagans have a better time of it than Christians, because they may at least remain naively within themselves and perfect themselves without temptations. As for Christians, however, apart from those few chosen ones whom you simply snatch up with violence and transfer into your world, the rest remain crucified in a pitiful sort of middle state and they are neither earthly nor heavenly.

At last I believed I understood. It cannot be otherwise, for all creatures are finite, they have their measure and their limits. And when this finitude encounters infinite love and its demands, it cannot but turn of itself into a prison. There is in finite beings a fear of being burst asunder by God, and this is why they close themselves off when approached. It is a pious error to think that we long for the infinite and for a liberation from our bonds. Experience contradicts this. Far from accepting from God the measure of infinity, we actually impose on him the measure of our finitude. Step by step we defend our ground with armed violence. We lay down our peace offer: Thus far am I willing to go, this much am I prepared to concede you. Be satisfied with it and do not trespass my bounds. You would only crush me utterly. You would overwind the spring in the clock. You must complete from the storehouses of your infinity what I lack. This far will I go: lure me no further! Know that the measure by which I judge myself is this definite "scale of perfections" which I have devised for myself, drawing on your clearly expressed prohibitions and supplementing these with a definite number of voluntary works of love. And I have set my will on the firm keeping of this principle: intentionally to pretend not to hear your unclear and amorphous call to the undefined which is above and beyond. Since I am only one member of your Church, it is sensible for you to expect only a part from me, and not the whole. It is up to you to build the totality of the City of God, using the many fragments of individuals! All human perfection does, indeed, lie in measure.

Finally, you yourself have created me to exist within a prison, the prison of this my ego. In it I live, move and have my being. And I love this ego, "for no one hates his own flesh." This space is familiar to me: my thought illumines it; my senses crowd it with the world's concerns; my will expands it widely. In this monad the universe is irretrievably reflected. Only within this interior space can I know the world, or even you: everything must be measured according to its standards. Just as the eye can see only colors and the ear can hear only sounds, so, too, I can know anything whatever only in its relationship to myself. Even love is a law of this ego: love is its fruitfulness, its creative inclination to what is other, the transcendence which is rooted in it. Even when its yearning seems to make the ego rattle the grill around it, even this belongs to its life and it makes the ego's existence richer and more love-worthy. This self, O God, is the highest and only gift which I received from your hand. And now you want to call it into question again, you even want to take it back from me again! But here I will certainly defend myself. No, I do not long to go outside of myself! What would be the good of an ecstasy of "coalescing" with nature or with a loved person, if I could no longer experience them? How could I make you a gift of my love or offer you my ego in love if I no longer have this ego, if I am dispossessed of myself? (And just this appears to be the secret goal of all your goading!) Leave me my ego and then you shall have it! This is my beloved dungeon: I yearn for no freedom! By long association I have grown fond of this prison-house of my sufferings with all its shortcomings and all its heavy burden. When nature demands it, take my body from me (you will, in any case, return it to me in beauty)—just do not rob me of my soul! You cannot exact the impossible feat that I should migrate out of myself, that I should become a stranger to myself and at midnight, like a thief, climb out of my own window—out into

141

a certain death! Do not, my Father, draw out your knife over me! "We do not want to be stripped down, but clothed over, that what is mortal may pass over into life!" If you tear my shells apart, like an oyster's, I shall be destroyed!

MY SON, between midnight and morning frost, when they dragged me to the second trial, I sojourned in your prison. I sat fettered to a tent-peg—lonely, beaten, disgraced—and I thought of you and of the rising day. I have tasted your prison; nothing of its bittersweet smell of decay was spared me. I have wandered through even the deepest chamber of all the prisons of all those who, in despair, have struggled against God's freedom. Down below in the lowest part of you, in the lightless disgrace of your impotence and your refusal, there have I chosen my abode. As a small root cracks the heaviest stones apart, so have I softly caused your prison walls to waver. You are still holding out against my love with the strength of your despair; but your arm is already beginning to flinch. Little by little you are yielding to my pressure.

I will not betray to you the secret by virtue of which I overcame your despair. Fatigued from his spiteful tears, the child finally falls asleep. By the following morning he has already forgotten his resistance and his disconsolate anguish. There is great magic in such extinguished memory: a new leaf is turned, a new chapter begins. Whether or not you are able is not the question at the moment. The whole point is that I have been able. When alone and locked up in yourself you brooded over your profound failure, you were strangely at variance within yourself: you were divided within yourself. Your unity—in that melancholy embrace of desire and regret—was mere illusion. Quietly, without your noticing it, I have cleaved you open and thus given you unity.

You no longer think of progress, and this is good. You would only have made progress towards yourself. Your steps would never have gone really ahead. But now leave your brooding aside. Let the dead bury what is dead. Turn your glance away from the misery of your fetters and fix it—a long, lingering glance—upon my misery. You will see what you did not want to believe. Your prison has become my prison and my freedom your freedom. Do not ask how this happened; but rejoice and give thanks. Even a corpse does not rot forever. It decomposes; water and worms carry off its stuff, and when the years have passed, in its place there lies a wholesome and fertile patch of earth. You are finite—that is true—and this is why your resistance also is finite, and finally I will bring you to terms. The tough pods fall to the ground like the protective leaves around blossoms. The armor bursts open and out crawls a butterfly. Blind and unconscious it clings to the edge of a leaf, while blood expands the lobes of its wings. When it feels they have become rigid and lustrous, without reflecting, automatically as it were, it leaves the stalk and begins its flight.

And what you have said about yourself is folly. You would not be my creature if you had not been created open. All love strives to go out of itself into

143

the immeasurable spaces of freedom. It seeks adventure and, in so doing, forgets itself. I do not say that you were able to free yourself, for it was for this that I have come. Nor am I saying that love's freedom lay contained within yourself, for I have given it to you. The Father has drawn you to me.

You are free. The angel nudged you on the side, the clamps fell from your wrists, the gate flew open on its own, and the two of you floated out past the sleeping guards until you reached freedom. You still think it was a dream. Rub the sleep out of your eyes. You are free to go wherever you please.

But look: many of your brothers are still languishing in prison. Are you going to enjoy your freedom while they suffer? Or do you want to help me loosen their shackles, and together with me to share their prison?

CHAPTER IX

A WOUND HAS BLOSSOMED

G O AWAY FROM ME! I am a sinful man. But why am
I still speaking with you? The breath from my
mouth reaches you like a poison and defiles you. Go
away and dissolve this impossible bond. There was a
time when I was a sinner like other sinners, a time
when I could still snatch up the gift of your grace, the
gift of my remorse, as the beggar catches the copper
penny thrown into his round hat. With it I could buy
myself bread and soup: I could live because of you. I
could taste the bliss of remorse. I could chew the bitter
herb of contrition as a benefit of your grace. Grace-
filled bitterness sweetened the bitterness of my guilt.
But today—what to do? Into what hole can I crawl so
that you will no longer see me, so that I will no longer
be a burden to you and that the decay of my person
may no longer importune you? I have sinned right to
your face, and the mouth which touched your lips—
your divine lips—a thousand times has kissed the lips
of the world and said: "I do not know him." I do not
know this man. If I knew him I would not have been
able to betray him thus—without hesitation, so natur-

ally. And if I perhaps did know him, then I certainly did not love him. For love cannot betray in such a way; it cannot turn away like that, with the most innocent of faces. Love cannot forget love. That I was able to forsake you like that after all that had happened between us proves only one thing: that I was not worthy of your love and that I myself never really possessed love. It is neither arrogance nor humility, but quite simply the truth, that now makes me say to you: "I've had enough." I do not want any further ray of your purity to stray into my hell. It is a beautiful thing when love condescends to what is base, but it is unbearable when love becomes base with the base. There is a betrayal that cannot be made up for. A residue remains for all eternity, and my eyes will never again be able to meet your eyes. I will fling the thirty silver pieces into the temple—but, please, do not confuse this deed with remorse. Such a high-sounding word does not fit here. My soul is sealing its lips tightly to keep any word from escaping. My deed is word enough: it cries up to heaven, but it would be better if it cried down to hell. Do me a last favor and turn away; I can no longer look on this spat-on face. Wash yourself off and leave me where I am, where I belong. This time I know who I am. And this time it's for good.

Surely you know what your Apostle has said: "It is no longer possible to awaken to remorse those who had once been enlightened, had tasted the gift from heaven, had received the Holy Spirit, had experienced God's glorious Word and the powers of the world to come then nonetheless have again fallen away. On their own they crucify the Son of God anew and make a mockery of him. If a piece of land drinks in the rain which abundantly pours down upon it and then produces the fruit desired by those who have worked it, that land receives God's blessing. But if it bears thistles and thorns, it is useless and accursed, and its end is fire." Enough of this manure around the fruitless tree, which I believe only wanted to prove to you that too much care does no good. Cut it down and not another word about it.

Men wounded your Heart; water and blood flowed out. Men drank and became healthy; they washed themselves and became pure. But I have done something very different. I have dealt a sharp blow at the heart of love. I have killed love. I have struck love's innermost marrow knowing what I was doing, and I have touched the most delicate nerve of love's life. It has collapsed into ruin; it is no longer. A corpse hangs on the Cross. I sit at a distance and brood in my lost infamy. I am the son of ruination.

I have used up your Cross and your mercy. Everything has been consumed, to the very last drop—even the return of the lost son and the lamb caught among the thorns and the lost drachma. Everything used up and worn out. One can play this scene twenty times over, fifty perhaps, but then it turns stale and loses its salt. Once again I hear your Apostle saying: When we sin intentionally with full knowledge of the truth, then there no longer is any sacrifice for our sins.

Rather, a horrible judgment and the blast of the fire await us which will destroy the adversaries. Whoever violates the law of Moses will be killed without mercy upon the testimony of two or three witnesses. How much heavier a punishment will overtake the one who tramples on the Son of God with his feet, who holds the blood of the Covenant, with which he has been sanctified, to be base, who scoffs at Grace. This you can calculate yourselves! We do indeed know the one who said: "Mine is vengeance! I want to avenge!" And further: "The Lord will judge his people. It is a terrible thing to fall into the hands of the living God."

There is a communion of saints, and there is also a communion of sinners. Perhaps they are both one and the same thing—this chain, this wave that rolls on through days and centuries, a bloody stream of guilt, the blunderers' course of those who drag themselves down and pull themselves up again. *One* life of warm guilt and of warm remorse throbs through them all, and amid this dark stream of good and evil suffering there flow also the redeeming drops of your blood, O Lord. You shall save them.

I have been expelled from this communion of sinners. Stiff and frozen, rolled up lump-like, I cower to the side: my sin is without comparison. When those others fail, the angel of God weeps in their midst. For me there is no angel. When they fall, a secret vessel bursts in them and bitter longing is poured out like a sacrifice. But in me nothing breaks any longer. Everything is hard and inexorably sealed off. When they have sinned they may still go on and pray. What prayer should I still be able to utter that would not be accompanied by hell's mocking laughter? How am I still supposed to believe what I say to you? "I am sorry." "I want to love you." I have proof from experience that this is not true. In the others the offended Holy Spirit still moans on. In me everything remains mute, and this, very likely, is what is called the sin against the Spirit. The others fall to their knees before the Cross. I've managed to get behind the Cross. The others persevere as men taught by God: "It was good that you humbled me, for thus I learned to know your justification." I have long since graduated from this school; in me sin no longer has any improving aspect. Sin in me is round and sated and unassailable from any side—a ball of fire and iron.

Leave me alone. Neither let your Mother touch me. I am no sight for you two. Do not waste your compassion on me: it would be misplaced. Let the inevitable come down upon me. To the one on your right up there you promised Paradise. I heartily concede it to him. He has earned it. He did not know what he was doing. Be happy together in your eternal garden! But don't torture yourself over me. I'll always be the one on your left. And stop torturing me too with your torture. Try to forget me.

WAS THAT LIGHTNING? Was the fruit on the Cross visible in the darkness for a flash as the sky was rent—motionless, stiff as death itself, with fixed, vacant eyes, pale as a maggot, probably already dead? That was indeed his body, but where is his soul? In what shoreless beaches, in what waterless depths of the sea, on the bottom of what dark flames does it drift about? Suddenly all of them standing around the gallows know it: he is gone. Immeasurable emptiness (not solitude) streams forth from the hanging body. Nothing but this fantastic emptiness is any longer at work here. The world with its shape has perished; it tore like a curtain from top to bottom, without making a sound. It fainted away, turned to dust, burst like a bubble. There is nothing more but nothingness itself. The world is dead. Love is dead. God is dead. Everything that was, was a dream dreamt by no one. The present is all past. The future is nothing. The hand has disappeared from the clock's face. No more struggle between love and hate, between life and death. Both have been equalized, and love's emptying out has become the emptiness of hell. One has penetrated the other perfectly. The nadir has reached the zenith: nirvana.

Was that lightning? Was the form of a Heart visible in the boundless void for a flash as the sky was rent, drifting in the whirlwind through the worldless chaos, driven like a leaf? Or was it winged, propelled and directed by its own invisible wings, standing as lone survivor between the soulless heavens and the perished earth?

Chaos. Beyond heaven and hell. Shapeless nothingness behind the bounds of creation. Is that God? God died on the Cross. Is that death? No dead are to be seen. Is it the end? Nothing that ends is any longer there. Is it the beginning? The beginning of what? In the beginning was the Word. What kind of word? What incomprehensible, formless, meaningless word? But look: What is this light glimmer that wavers and begins to take form in the endless void? It has neither content nor contour. A nameless thing, more solitary than God, it emerges out of pure emptiness. It is no one. It is anterior to everything. Is it the beginning? It is small and undefined as a drop. Perhaps it is water. But it does not flow. It is not water. It is thicker, more opaque, more viscous than water. It is also not blood, for blood is red, blood is alive, blood has a loud human speech. This is neither water nor blood. It is older than both, a chaotic drop. Slowly, slowly, unbelievably slowly the drop begins to quicken. We do not know whether this movement is infinite fatigue at death's extremity or the first beginning—of what? Quiet, quiet! Hold the breath of your thoughts! It's still much too early in the day to think of hope. The seed is still much too weak to start whispering about love. But look there: it is indeed moving, a weak, viscous flow. It's still much too early to speak of a wellspring. It trickles, lost in the chaos, direction-less, without gravity. But more copiously now. A wellspring in the chaos. It leaps out of pure nothing-ness, it leaps out of itself. It is not the beginning of God, who eternally and mightily brings himself into existence as Life and Love and triune Bliss. It is not the beginning of creation, which gently and in slumber slips out of the Creator's hands. It is a beginning without parallel, as if Life were arising from Death, as if weariness (already such weariness as no amount of sleep could ever dispel) and the uttermost decay of power were melting at creation's outer edge, were beginning to flow, because flowing is perhaps a sign and a likeness of weariness which can no longer contain itself, because everything that is strong and solid must in the end dissolve into water. But hadn't it—in the beginning—also been born from water? And is this wellspring in the chaos, this trickling weariness, not the beginning of a new creation?

The magic of Holy Saturday. The chaotic fountain remains directionless. Could this be the residue of the Son's love which, poured out to the last when every vessel cracked and the old world perished, is now making a path for itself to the Father through the glooms of nought? Or, in spite of it all, is this love trickling on in impotence, unconsciously, laboriously, towards a new creation that does not yet even exist, a creation which is still to be lifted up and given shape? Is it a protoplasm producing itself in the beginning, the first seed of the New Heaven and the New Earth? The spring leaps up even more plenteously. To be sure, it flows out of a wound and is like the blossom and fruit of a wound; like a tree it sprouts up from this wound. But the wound no longer causes pain. The suffering has been left far behind as the past origin and previous source of today's wellspring. What is poured out here is no longer a present suffering, but a suffering that has been concluded—no longer now a sacrificing love, but a love sacrificed. Only the wound is there: gaping, the great open gate, the chaos, the nothingness out of which the wellspring leaps forth. Never again will this gate be shut. Just as the first creation arose ever anew out of sheer nothingness, so, too, this second world—still unborn, still caught up in its first rising—will have its sole origin in this wound, which is never to close again. In the future, all shape must arise out of this gaping void, all wholeness must draw its strength from the creating wound. High-vaulted triumphal Gate of Life! Armored in gold, armies of graces stream out of you with fiery lances. Deep-dug Fountain of Life! Wave upon wave gushes out of you inexhaustible, ever-flowing, billows of water and blood baptizing the heathen hearts, comforting the yearning souls, rushing over the deserts of guilt, enriching over-abundantly, overflowing every heart that receives it, far surpassing every desire.

PART THREE

THE VICTORY

CHAPTER X

ROSE OF SORROWS

N O ONE SAW THE HOUR OF YOUR VICTORY. No one
is witness to the birth of a world. No one knows
how the night of that Saturday's hell was transformed
into the light of the Easter dawn. Asleep it was that we
were all carried on wings over the abyss, and asleep did
we receive the grace of Easter. And no one knows how
it happened to him. No one knows which hand it was
caressed his cheek so that suddenly the wan world
beamed with a thousand colors, and he had to smile
involuntarily over the miracle that was realized in him.

Who can describe what it means to say: "The Lord
is Spirit"? Spirit is the invisible reality that asserts itself more manifestly than all that is sensible. Spirit is
the invisible fragrance of the Paradise that has arisen
in our very midst. Spirit is the great invisible wing
which we recognize by the blowing of the wind and
by the keen desire that overflows us when we are but
grazed by its down. Spirit is the Paraclete, the Consoler, whose tenderness makes the word of remorse
be muted unsaid, absorbed like a drop of dew in the
sunlight. A great white mantle, light as silk, is laid

about your body, and under it the clinging garments of despair fall to tatters of themselves. Spirit is a sorcerer: it can create in you what does not exist; it can make disappear what appeared to be irremovable; in the midst of a wilderness it creates gardens, fountains, birds; and what it conjures is no specter: it is sheer truth. And along with the truth it creates faith for you. You believe the Word: you see it, perceive it, touch it. You feel the new faculty that has sprung up in you. You run your hand over the smooth skin from which the wound has vanished by a miracle. You live in the realm of miracles, you go about as children do in a fairy-tale—in bliss and as a matter of course. All of your past is like a dream which one can no longer recall precisely, and the entire old world hangs within the new space like a picture in its frame.

Only a while ago you still knelt at the empty grave, a sea of tears. And all you knew was that the Lord was dead, that the life of quiet joy you shared was dead. You only stare into the void of the cave. A cold and chilly wind is exhaled from your soul, where the dead man laid himself to rest, where you embalmed and shrouded him with an awe that no longer expects anything. You want to be in attendance at his grave. You don't cease praying or going to empty ceremonies in churches, to perform a hopeless service for your dead love. And oh, what is now the meaning of resurrection? Who can know it from among those who have not themselves risen from the dead? What is now the meaning of faith? It has been sealed within the grave. What is now the meaning of hope? A leaden thought with neither power nor yearning. And love? Alas, perhaps it is now no more than sorrow, the empty pain of disconsolate futility, the weariness that can no longer mourn. And so you stare into the void. For in fact: the grave is empty, you are yourself empty, and are, therefore, already pure, and only this staring spasm keeps you from looking behind you. You stare ahead of you, and behind your back stands your Life! It calls to you, you turn around and cannot recognize it. Your eyes, unused to light, can grasp nothing. And then an abrupt word: your name! Your own dear name coming from the mouth of Love: your being, your very essence—yourself!—bounding from the mouth thought dead . . . O word, O name, you, my own name! Spoken to me, breathed forth with a smile and a promise. O stream of light, O faith, hope, love! In a thunderclap I am the new creature (this I am, can be, am allowed to be). I am given back to myself, and then, at the very instant when I shout for joy, I cast myself down at the feet of Life.

"I am the Resurrection and the Life!" Whoever believes in me, whomever I touch, whoever hears his name from my mouth, is alive and has risen from the dead. And today is your Last Day (your youngest day), the newest, most childlike of days. No other day will ever be as young for you as this today, when Eternal Life has called you by name.

Now I know who I am, and now I *may* be who I am, for my love loves me, my love has bestowed trust on me. This Now when our two names have met is my birthday in eternity, and no time shall ever erase this Now. Here is where the starting point has been set. Here is creation and new beginning. Here is where the bell is cast into the empty mold. The rigid envelope which enclosed me from the outside and preserved my emptiness now shatters to fragments, and from this point on I will be able to peal from high towers and proclaim, *proclaim*! "Go and announce it to my brothers!" Already I see your wings beating impatiently. Go, my dove, my Easter messenger, proclaim it to your brothers. For in this do resurrection and life consist: in further proclaiming the Good News, in carrying on the flame, in being a useful instrument in my hand that I may build up my Kingdom in men's hearts, in letting my Heart go on beating in yours. And even if they don't believe you, just as you yourself did not believe, nevertheless, because Life has illuminated you, Life's power of convincing will shine forth from you, too, and will turn their stiffened senses around.

Go forth and proclaim! And while she dashes off, the Lord's Spirit begins to blow, and all about it flashes forth in despondent souls as from a gladsome sky, and in that instant it lifts them up erect and casts the same fire into them. And when they, drunk with happiness, try to grasp him with eyes and hands, he sends them on their way even while disappearing: "Go forth and proclaim!" And he whirls them towards one another in a breathless whirlwind. And, finally, in the evening they stood in the room all aglow and, full of his love, they spoke animatedly with each other, and while they were still speaking, behold: there he stood in their midst and greeted them: "Peace be with you!"

The peace which the world neither knows nor can give. The peace which transcends all speculation and imaginings in such a supereminently high and deep and compelling manner that their heart would have collapsed for sheer over-abundance if what he was giving them was not, precisely, *peace*. O tidal wave of silence! O storm of calm! God's Paradise is so simple that it consists of a meal of honeycomb and baked fish. So earthly is his Paradise that it is a fisherman's morning at the Lake of Genesareth. The waves splash, the first rays of the sun shimmer through the fog. On the beach stands a man calling out and making signs. The nets are cast out on the right and at once they are teeming with a full catch. On the shore breakfast is ready. They all recline on the ground while the nets dry out, and, since no one needs to ask who this stranger is, the waves splash against the silence. O peace beyond all questioning: It is the Lord! Everything is as simple as if things had never been otherwise. The Master blesses the bread, as always, and hands it to them after he has broken it. As if the Cross, the darkness, death itself had never been. "Peace be with you!" As if treachery, denial, and curses had never welled up in their hearts. "Peace be with you! Not as the world gives it do I give it to

161

you. Let not your heart be anxious and shudder. For see: I have overcome the world."

And you, Simon Peter, son of John: Do you love me? Do you love me, O soul who betrayed me three times? Have you not always loved me, and was it not love when you came furtively after me instead of fleeing like the others into safe little corners? Was it not love when you stood at the soldiers' camp that night—freezing and out of your senses, disconnected and paralyzed? You were warming yourself; but what warmth penetrated into your torpid soul that denied without knowing how this was happening. It denied because all of you had to abandon me so that I could go my way alone, a way that only the solitary treads. It denied only because the bitter torrent of tears at cock-crow was to make it fully my own. All this is now distant and hardly even perceptible. A new leaf has been turned. I have overcome not only death, and not only sin, but sin's disgrace no less, its scarlet infamy, the bitter dregs of your guilt and your remorse and your bad conscience. Look: all this has vanished, leaving less trace than does the snow when it melts under the Easter sun. You look with such candor into my eyes, with such freedom and such an innocent mien—not even with the dissembling of the young boy who wants to hide his prank behind a naive face. Your gaze upon me is more nimble than a spring song and your glance to the very bottom is as blue as the sky above us. And so I must indeed believe you when you say: "Yes, Lord. You know that I love you." This is my Easter present to you: your good conscience; and with a good conscience must you accept this gift, for on the day of my victory I will not tolerate a sullen heart. What are you then to do with this broken-heartedness you've outgrown, this stillborn attempt to appear miserable? Leave to the Pharisees this precise and just balancing of guilt and remorse, the weight of your sin and the length and intensity of your feelings of guilt: all this belongs in the Old Covenant. I have borne guilt and shame and bad conscience. The New Covenant is now born with the innocence of Paradise and through rebirth in water and the Holy Spirit. So overpowering is the radiance of this new-born world that your soul is not capable of experiencing the feelings of the past, decayed world, even if it should attempt to experience them "against the grain," so to speak. Can the calyx of a flower put up resistance when the sun innundates it with such floods of warmth and light? Can it remain closed because it is not perhaps worthy of looking this holy light in the eye? If parents forgive their children and friends forgive one another—and these are but human beings who cannot create—how should I, your Creator, not be able to accomplish this creative deed in the dawn of my Resurrection?

So you, too, come up, Thomas. Come forth from your cave of sorrows. Put your finger here and see my hands. Extend your hand and place it in my side. And do not think that your blind suffering is more clair-voyant than my grace. Do not embattle yourself in

163

the fortress of your torments. You naturally believe you see more clearly than the others. You have proofs in hand. You see yourself—your old man—black and white, and everything in you cries out: "Impossible!" You see the distance and can measure with accuracy the gap between misdeeds and atonement, the gap between you and me. Who could struggle against such evidence? You withdraw into your sorrow: this, at least, is yours. In the experience of your woes you feel yourself alive. And if someone should lay a hand to your sorrows and attempt to tear them up by the root, surely he would tear your whole heart out of your breast—so intertwined have you and your sufferings become. Nevertheless, I have risen. And your wise pain, your senile pain, into which you gladly plunge, by which you think you show me fidelity, through which you believe you are united to me: your pain is an anachronism. For today I am young and utterly happy. And what you call your fidelity is nothing but obstinacy. Do you have the standard in your hand? Is your soul the arbiter of what might be possible for God? Is your heart, swollen with experiences, the clock from which you tell what God's decree for you might be? What you take to be profundity is but unbelief. But since you are so wounded and the open torment of your heart has opened up to the abyss of your very self, put out your hand to me and, with it, feel the pulse of another Heart: through this new experience your soul will surrender and heave up the dark gall which it has long collected. I must overpower you. I cannot spare exacting from you your melancholy—your most-loved possession. Give it to me, even if it costs you your soul and your inner self thinks it must die. Give me this idol, this cold stony clot in your breast, and in its place I will give you a new heart of flesh that will beat to the pulse of my own Heart. Give me this self of yours, which lives on its not being able to live, which is sick because it cannot die. Let it perish, and you will finally begin to live. You are enamoured of the sad puzzle of your incomprehensible ego. But you have already been seen through and comprehended, for look: if your heart accuses you, I am nevertheless greater than this your heart, and I know everything. Dare to make the leap into the Light! Do not take the world to be more profound than God! Do not think that I cannot make short work of you! Your city is besieged, your provisions are exhausted: you must capitulate. What could be simpler and sweeter than opening the door to love? What could be easier than falling to one's knees and saying: "My Lord and my God!"?

MY KINGDOM GROWS IN ALL OF YOU. You do not see this Kingdom, or you only have distant inklings of it in bits and pieces. But I am the King and the center of all hearts, and the innermost and best-kept secret of all hearts is to me an open book. You see but the outer wrapping by which men conceal themselves from one another. I look into souls from the inside, from that center to which they stand open,

165

defenselessly. And there, at their innermost, is where their true face is to be found. There is where their gold glitters; there the hidden pearl lies. There gleam the Image and the Likeness, the signs of nobility imprinted upon them. There is where the eyes are open that perpetually behold the face of the Father. There the lamp keeps watch before the tabernacle, even when the body and the exterior soul slumber. In that interior chamber there is something pure, something stirring and well-intentioned, which corresponds to what men try to accomplish externally in an awkward, inept and often perverted manner. And when they really love and do good to one another, their inner countenance also beams and smiles upon me, and I receive more than do their human brothers. Everything good in them—which they themselves ignore and perhaps through a kind of shame, do not want to know—is turned toward me. The inconceivable beauty of souls, which my father has hidden from them so that they do not become enamoured of the creaturely mirror: this beauty, which next to God's is the most awe-inspiring, stands unveiled before my eyes. Do you not think it is wonderful to see all of this, to see how these millions of hearts, which only I can count, open up in a gigantic sphere like a huge rose of sorrows all about my own Heart, laboriously breathing up toward the light? So much struggle, so much exposure, so much blind daring, so much frantic search for help and, always, constant anguish, obstacles, hesitations, stumblings, fallings, getting up again, continuing down the road: and all of it towards me. Every individual life is an interminably interlocked chain, a story which must every moment be invented anew, an enticement, a vague promise, a presentiment, then a sudden insight, a decision made in a still half-veiled manner, a course as real as a dream, and then again dusk, fog, a sudden standstill (the thought that perhaps it would be preferable after all to live on one's own), steps in reverse, puzzlement, a slight discouragement but—what was that? My voice perhaps? A listening, a reflecting, a repenting, or maybe also deliberate disregard of the voice: a spiteful stepping to the side, where one lies down and plays dead for years, perhaps, until a new summons strikes the ear like lightning—an abrupt, convulsive jolt out of one's sleep and then one hastily takes to the road again alarmed by so much lost time. And all of this multiplied a thousandfold, again and again, every single time, in a wholly new manner with each soul: a world in transition, the Kingdom in the act of becoming, the heavenly Jerusalem under construction, the migration of the peoples to Paradise—and always with me as their goal. And every soul a gift of the Father to me. I may turn to each one, squander myself for each one, spread myself out as a road under his feet, rise high over destiny's every avenue as the Gate of Life. Between every soul and me there is this covenant, this virginal bond of holy marriage. For each one I am the whole, the utmost, the unconditional. I am father, mother, friend and spouse. For each one I am there as ready fulfillment when all endearing illusions, all false lovers have finally failed. Again and again there unfolds the scene with the broken alabaster jar, the tears and the loosened hair: someone pours his life out before me like a pound of genuine aromatic nard or like a snapped string of pearls. Or the episode at Jacob's well, or at Simon the Pharisee's, or the unforgettable conversation with that woman at the Temple or the look of the one leper who came back to thank me, or of the young man when he awoke from the dead there on his bier: he looked around when he was outside the city and stared back at the people who were staring at him, and he saw his mother, and then me last of all, and very slowly he began to understand; or the sight of my friend, John, at the foot of the Cross when he clung to me with every fiber of his being and offered his entire soul up to me like a vase; or, finally, my life with my Mother, never to be exhausted: sitting upon her lap, growing up to her stature, her gradual transformation into friend and bride. And all of this offered to me (O homage!) since the beginning of the world, for the Patriarchs too thirsted to witness my day, and they did so and were consoled by it. Later came the innumerable host of saints who, going down the equally winding paths of grace, were prevailed upon by me to surrender their entire soul. But there are also others, those in the mist further below who are less favored by the Father's sun. On laborious paths they trudge on up towards me, gasping under their burden of guilt and of a fate scarcely to be improved. These are the little people, the tawdry populace that extends like a herd beyond reach of the eye. Few among them know what is happening, most of them are made dull by the darkness, and they do not know me. To their blind eyes I am only a blurred brightness (as with that blind man whom I healed and who, when I first touched him, said: "I see people going about like trees"). But if they should see the least glimmer, they're already smiling and they again begin to plod forward readily. Everything, however, which men endeavor and invent is mine and is aimed towards me as to their center, and none of it is lost from my Kingdom. Whatever they glimpsed in my original design and translated into statues, houses, bridges; whatever they took from my voice's resonance and transformed into music; whatever they caught from my white light and separated into color and contour (and often people have wept over the beautiful, but only because through it I touched their heart without their knowing it); whatever their creative instinct has caught up from a deeper center as "the work," and in the artist's plan aimed at a higher, an infinitely higher goal than this pitiful rough draft or these dull lines have been able to convey: all of this must, in its invisible prolongation, be aimed at a middle-point within myself. And everything that men have accomplished in the way of community and mutual relief through their federations, states and nations has been devised with me implicitly in mind: all of it is a shadow of the

169

City with the twelve pearl gates and it provides me with stones and beams for the building of my Kingdom.

And even in their idols must they serve me. Those that deny and persecute me are, in effect, madly searching out my tracks in the refuse heap of their own enlightened ideals. For all men I am the Way, the Truth and the Life, even when they do not know the road on which they are travelling and have no idea of where it is leading them, even when to them the truth is but a debris of puzzles and what they call "life" but a feeble echo and a distorted reflection of life in me. How often I have trodden that road to Emmaus, as companion of those who have not recognized me or even heard my name. But their hearts burned while I explained to them the Book of Life, and (why shouldn't I say it?) my own Heart burned for sheer joy at the pilgrimage.

And then there's my presence with the poor. Uncertain of the next day, they lie down in rags within their hovels, torn between complaint and surrender. At that moment before they fall asleep, I am there to caress their soul with an invisible hand, to wipe away their involuntary and, oh, so understandable resistance against the will of the Father, and to open them up to the fullness of painful patience. And on stormy mornings I accompany them on their way to the factory, on their way to a joyless workday, which in its rigor so closely resembles my own. I walk through hospital wards and visit my brothers who through their suffering cooperate in my work, though without knowing it. I pass over battlefields where life, as it is ending, is three steps away from Paradise and yet is all convulsed in the spasms of death. I traverse the breadth and length of sin's underworld—the sewers of depravity and despair—and my passing soothes. Along the way I discover many a jewel that, covered with refuse, awaits the liberating fire. Whatever I touch receives sight; what I bless becomes pure; what I gaze upon begins to look up with hope. I disappoint no one: I am rich enough to fill up every void, joyful enough to surpass every worldly joy, powerful enough to snatch to myself even the most outcast. My Kingdom is unbounded and superabundant: how should I not love it? Who does not love his own body? But it is the Church which is this Body, and, through her, the world as well. Who would not die with a merry heart for such a bride? For everything which was created in me—and without me nothing has come to be—is a womb for the seed of my Word and a chaste mouth for my Kiss.

And yet, even this is not my ultimate bliss. My Kingdom is not my Kingdom. Everything that belongs to me belongs to the Father. I love you, all of my created brethren, for my Father's sake. You are the booty that I bring home in my triumphal procession and cast down before his throne. Believe me: the Father loves you. He loves you so much that he did not spare me, but delivered me up for you. He is the Doer: I was but his Deed. It is he who has planned, created and established. It is he who elected, predestined and loved you when you were still sinners. It is he who has drawn you to himself so that, filled with his grace, you should go and proclaim the greatness of his might. His is the Kingdom, and you should therefore pray thus: "May your Kingdom come to us. It is your will, not mine, which should be done." I place back in his hands the Kingdom which I established with anguish and blood, the Kingdom which has been founded today, on this Easter. I spread it out before his feet as my homage. The bliss of a man who has conquered a kingdom with the sword, then to present it to his bride as a gift: what is it compared with the bliss I experience at handing over the universal cosmos to the Father? For surely every best gift comes down from the Father of Lights, and nothing can be given to him which he has not himself previously conferred on the giver. And I, too—the reflected splendor of his glory, the mirror of his Being—I am only through him. When he embraces me in the Holy Spirit and, with me, all his creation, what is he then receiving if not what he himself had first poured forth? He is the fountain of all good. Thus, it is my happiness to be his possession and the ray of his light; it is my happiness continually to return to his bosom through the gloomy world. And yet, I return home richer than when I set out. Does not the Holy Spirit, in whom we are united, proceed from both of us? Would the Godhead be perfect if I did not breathe him forth? And does not the world also, in me, participate in this creation in a creaturely way? Should not the world, which is gift to itself, also approach the all-giving Father with full hands? Should not the seed of the Kingdom bring in fruit sixty- and a hundredfold—a full harvest—since it has first been given a power all its own? Like the ray which is caught between two mirrors, so does my happiness vibrate between two delights. The first is to possess nothing of my own, nothing that does not belong to my Father, even within my person to be his gift to myself, so that in everything I am I encounter only his goodness. The second is to be allowed to build him the Kingdom with my own power, with the pain and the death which he himself did not experience, and, in the Holy Spirit who proceeds from both of us, to be able to hand over to him the solid universe like a hard crystal in the sun. Both these things are bliss: To vanish in order to let him alone appear, to appear as his Word in order to proclaim him. I and the world are trapped in this play of love's waves, and nothing is left now but the greater honor of the ever-greater Father.

CHAPTER XI

AND THE SEA OF BEING LAY DRY

T HOMAS, YOU HAVE PLUNGED YOUR FINGER into my open Heart. Has your soul also felt what I mean when I say: "I am meek and humble of Heart"? Have you, my disciple, guessed at this innermost secret of my Heart, a secret that I truly take to heart and which fills it to the brim? O my friends! If you had understood this, would you be treading that unending road to Emmaus filled with a confused spirit and in dull distress? Would you be breaking your heads, asking why I had to suffer and die, why my Kingdom does not appear, why your hope—your childish hope—was shattered like a toy and (since you can't stop repairing it daily) why it is daily shattered anew? Look: it is I myself who am shattering this hope of yours in a speedy kingdom, with thrones right and left, the trappings of grandeur, a triumphalist Church that reigns over all peoples from the rising of the sun to its setting: your hope in what you call the peace of Christ in the Kingdom of Christ, but which is only your longing for tranquillity and a secure existence in the kingdom of this world. You want to see my Resurrection in black and white, Thomas. You want to see it, and not to believe it, this Kingdom. You want to see the wounds instead of feeling them, instead of wresting the victory of the Kingdom by suffering with me.

Where did I triumph if not on the Cross? Are you as blind as the Jews and the pagans to think that Golgotha was my downfall and my failure? Do you believe it was only later—three days later—that I recovered from my death and climbed up laboriously from the pit of Hades to appear among you once again? Look: this is my secret, and there is no other in heaven or on earth: My Cross is salvation, my Death is victory, my Darkness is light. At that time, when I hung in torment and dread rushed into my soul because of the forsakenness, rejectedness, uselessness of my suffering, and all was gloomy, and only the seething rage of that mass of teeth hissed up mockingly at me, while heaven kept silence, shut tight as the mouth of a scoffer (but through the open gates of my hands and feet my blood bubbled out in spurts, and with each throb my Heart became more desolate, strength poured out from me in streams and there remained only faintness, death's fatigue, infinite failure), and at last I neared that mysterious and final spot on the very edge of being, and then—the fall into the void, the capsizing into the bottomless abyss, the vertigo, the finale, the un-becoming: that colossal death which only I have died. Through my death this has been spared you, and no one will ever experience what it really means to die: This was my victory.

While I was falling and did nothing but fall, the New World was emerging. While I was feeble beyond all conceivable weakness, my Bride, the Church, was growing strong. While I was losing myself, wholly delivering myself up, while I was forsaking the chamber of my person and without any refuge (not even in God) was being driven out of the most secret corner of myself, then was I awakening in my brethren's heart. Haven't I told you that if the grain of seed falls into the ground and dies it bears much fruit? For without dying it would remain alone. But what occurs in such a death? The grain ceases to be a grain. The root uses up this little storehouse of life, and the shoots consume it altogether. And when, over the course of the year, the full ear of corn comes to undulate through wind and sun, what is left of the grain of seed? Who thinks of the dark growth in the black, humid earth when he runs his fingers over the golden tresses? The kernel is consumed but has been resurrected in the ear of corn: it is itself and yet not itself. And this occurs a million times over on every field, and year after year. Such is the parable of my Kingdom and of my love.

But you, my children, what do you want? I see you equipped with ladders, striving to climb up high, to climb up at any cost. You are short of stature and you climb up on a tree to see me, and often I *am* the tree. One of your ladders is called prayer, contemplating reflection. By these means you think you will grasp me. Another you call virtue. It has many high rungs

176

and on this ladder of virtues you clamber up nimbly, casting furtive glances at each other to see who's better at it. You have even expounded upon humility as a virtue, and you practice it like people practice handholds. You constantly have on your lips my sacred words of mortification, interior poverty, patience in suffering, also the holy example I set for you of crib and cross. The smallest hardship you call a cross, and the most matter-of-course renunciation a sacrifice. You use even my Cross as a ladder to make your own wishes prevail. And perhaps you suffer only in order to be all the more effective later on. The power of the Church also enters your ambitions. You want to see her great and beauteous and all-encompassing, and even if you do not yourselves rule, you look on with satisfaction when the Church tends the throngs like a herd. How acute is this drive to power in you! How greatly it lives on secretly in all those who have died to the world for my name's sake! How sweet the song of the ancient serpent: "You will have knowledge and be like gods!" And many a one seeks the last place only because, in a more secret sense, it is the first. Consider this: Don't you experience disappointment when the world forgets to applaud your humility? How obsessed you are with your spiritual worth! And you assess men's religion according to whether they bow to you or not. You seek after holiness, which is a sign that you do not have it. The saint (which is what I am) does not strive after it. Unwitting, unconcerned, paying no heed to himself, the saint falls down before his brothers to wash their tired feet. Forgetting his own hunger for God, he seats them at table and goes about waiting on them.

Of whom was I thinking when, as a freezing child, I lay in the crib, if not of you? Of what did I speak in the splendor of Tabor with Moses and Elias, if not of my suffering for you? For whom did I ask the Father for signs, if not for you? For whose sake did I stumble my way through fourteen endless stations, if not for yours? And my divinity and the embrace of my Father: for whom did I leave these if not for you? You want to follow me? You want to be called my disciples? Then let that mind be yours which animated me: being God in my very substance, I did not cling to my equality with God, but rather emptied and annulled myself. I took on the figure of a slave, becoming wholly like men and descending below myself in men's everyday appearance, in bondage unto death, unto death on the Cross. You say to me: "Master, you came from above. You were rich and could gain nothing. You were God. How could you have longed for the divine life? But we are puny. Everything in us yearns for more. Our desire to possess God is the innate drive of us creatures. Those of you who speak in this way do not know to what spirit you belong. You are greedy for Godlikeness? Then look at me. Then walk in my way. You think I could gain nothing because I was already God? Is this the God I have revealed to you? The self-sufficient God of the wise men of this world, who lacks nothing? My love for you has put their philosophy to shame. For to be God was not enough for me. In my fullness I believed I missed your wants and I wanted to prove my divinity to you in no way other than by letting go of it in order to become your slave. Why do you try to bypass me to reach the Father? I am the path of *dhamma*, and besides me there is no other. I am the door. Whoever climbs over the wall is a thief, even if he should steal the heavenly life for himself.

This was the most divine thing about God (and to show this was my whole concern): God was free enough to give himself up. You call your urge for fulfillment love. But who knows the essence of love if not God, since God is love? Love is not that you have loved him, but that he has loved you and has given up his very soul for you, his brothers. His eternal bliss consisted of taking delight in squandering himself by a futile love for you. His unity, belonging to another world, consisted in multiplying himself a thousandfold in the mystery of Bread and Wine like the snow or the sand of the sea, all to nourish you with divine life. This was his self-sufficiency: that he began to hunger and to thirst and that, in the person of his members, he suffered every sort of poverty and disgrace and imprisonment and nakedness and disease. This, my brothers, was his victory: that I was able to defeat even my divinity and that in the slave's form I was able to manifest the Lord, and in sin's likeness the essence of love. That, being outside of God, I knew how to be in God. That I became all in everything I was not.

Understand what it means to give oneself away. To strip oneself of one's freedom out of freedom; and out of love, no longer to be free or to be lord over oneself; no longer to be able to determine where the journey will take you; to surrender oneself, to deliver oneself over to the series of consequences that carry us off in a direction we did not want—where to? You leap down from a high cliff. The leap is freely made, and yet, the moment you leap, gravity leaps upon *you*, and you tumble exactly like a dead stone to the very bottom of the gorge. This is how I decided to give myself. To give myself right out of my hand. To whom? It did not matter. To sin, to the world, to all of you, to the devil, to the Church, to the Kingdom of Heaven, to the Father . . . I wanted to be the one given away par excellence. The corpse over which the vultures gather. The Consumed, the Eaten, the Drunk, the Spilled, the Poured Out. The Plaything. The Worn Out. The one squeezed to the very dregs. The one trod upon to infinity. The one run over. The one thinned to air. The one liquified into an ocean. The Dissolved. This was the plan; this was the will of the Father. By fulfilling it through obedience (the fulfillment itself was obedience), I have filled the world from heaven down to hell, and every knee must bend before me, and all tongues must confess me. Now I am all in all, and this is why the death which poured me out is my victory. My descent, my vertiginous collapse, my going under (under myself) into everything that was foreign and contrary to God—down into the underworld: this was the ascent of this world into me, into God. My victory.

You are in God—at the price of my own Godhead. You have love—I lost it to you. This loss is my Kingdom. My Kingdom is not of this world, but the world is within my realm. When on the Cross my Heart was sweating in the wine-press, when all strength had already been surrendered and only the emptiness and the impotence still suffered; when all it could yield, drop by drop, was "I can't any more," and "I hardly have the will"; when all blood had abandoned the Heart and all spirit the soul: then it was only nothingness that bled, only the water of perfect exhaustion that still flowed when the lance bored in (visibly into the Heart of flesh, and invisibly into soul, spirit and God): in me God himself became exhausted. The Inexhaustible was exhausted. Life was lived out. Love was loved out.

This was my victory. In the Cross was Easter. In death the grave of the world was burst open. In the leap into the void was the ascension to heaven. Now I fill the world, and at last every soul lives from my dying. And wherever a man decides to forsake himself, to give up his own narrowness, his self-will, his power, his blockaded resistance to me, there my Kingdom flourishes. And yet, men can accomplish this only against their own will, and they prefer anything to being delivered over to my grace. For this reason I must go with them long distances, life-long distances, until they come to realize the truth, until they understand that they don't understand, and they open up their cramped fingers and let themselves fall back into my Heart. Until they feel the ground so falter beneath them that they do not make this groundlessness into a new platform, a new standpoint, or reduce this openness to a higher form of imprisonment, or form abandonment into a cleverer sort of protection, or make of God's foolishness a sublimer kind of wisdom. Until they have grown so unaccustomed to looking at themselves that they at last look at me as if for the first time. Until, afar off, the horizon of the Kingdom begins to dawn for those who seemed to know all about Christianity. Until grown weary of their own maturity and calculations, they understand for the first time the words: "Unless you become like little children . . . " Children are defenseless. Children drift about on the tides of their soul like pilotless skiffs. When a child weeps, it weeps totally. It abandons itself freely to its own tears and cannot dam up its sadness. It possesses no refuge in a tower to which it can flee to escape this flood. It weeps as long as it must, just as the heavens rain until the clouds are empty. And when a child rejoices it transforms itself wholly into joy. It lives its joy through and through, without bounds or reflections. And when it is afraid, it becomes unalloyed fear. It is not clever enough (O deadly cleverness!) to erect a glass wall between the horror and its own soul. The wise men of this world proclaim to you: "Blessed is he who possesses an asbestos chamber where neither the water nor the fire of life can assail him. Blessed is he who has so trained and restrained his passions that they form an uncrossable rampart around his citadel, making it unassailable to destiny." But I say to you: "Blessed is he who exposes himself to an existence never brought under mastery, who does not transcend but, rather, abandons himself to my ever-transcending grace. Blessed are not the enlightened whose every question has been answered and who are delighted with their own sublime light, the mature and ripe ones whose one remaining action is to fall from the tree: blessed, rather, are the chased, the harassed who must daily stand before my enigmas and cannot solve them. Blessed are the poor in spirit, those who lack a spirit of cleverness. Woe to the rich, and woe doubly to the rich in spirit!" Although nothing is impossible with God, it is difficult for the Spirit to move their fat heart. The poor are willing and easy to direct. Like little puppies they do not take their eyes from their master's hand to see if *perhaps* he may throw them a little morsel from his plate. So carefully do the poor follow my promptings that they listen to the wind (which blows where it pleases), even when it changes. From the sky they can read the weather and interpret the signs of the times. My grace is unpretentious, but the poor are satisfied with little gifts. This is why I have invited to my banquet the poor, the beggars, the crippled and the lame, and all those who with good humor have withdrawn to the furthest margin of decent society: tramps and highwaymen from the open road, all the world's ragamuffins and riffraff of fence-jumpers. These are my cherished, respected guests, and it is a pleasure for me to move among them. I cultivate familiar relations with tax-collectors and whores, for these will go before you into the Kingdom of Heaven. Simon, do you see that woman over there? She's an ordinary hussy, and yet she has loved much and kept little for herself, and for this reason much—everything—has been forgiven her, and I send her off with my peace as a gift.

I want to pour my fullness into empty vessels. To strike the roots of new hope into hopeless hearts. To place the child of the promise in Sarah's unfruitful womb. What should your piety mean to me, the affectation of your "spiritual life"? Compassion is what I want, and not holocausts. You strive for perfection, and this is a good thing. But do not be perfect other than as your Father in heaven, who makes his sun rise over both the just and the unjust, who makes it rain upon the good and the bad, who gives the servants of the eleventh hour the same denarius he gives those who have toiled from the first hour. You strive for perfection. This is a good thing; but I ask you: to what end? Because your brothers' salvation urges you on? Because the scandal they take inflames you? Because you want to sacrifice yourselves in your love's impulse to help? You seek to prepare your heart. Is it that it may be spotless, as the law requires for the lamb and the ram which are consumed by fire in place of the sin of the people? And you sense it: As long as my own heart clings to the gold of this world, how are my brothers to believe me when I proclaim poverty to them? And, so long as my body performs the works of the flesh, how is it to radiate the chastity for which my brothers so yearn? And so long as my spirit revels in its well-earned personal freedom, how can it speak credibly of the Lord's world-redeeming obedience? All these works should be for you a means to prepare yourselves as a means and an instrument of love. For, if you should have acquired all perfection and filled your heavenly granaries up to the very roof with merits, and had not love, it would all be of no use to you.

But how easy it is to have this love, don't you think? Look at the world and see it with my eyes. See how it exerts itself for vain things, how it greedily clutches its poisons, how it becomes addled with despair. See the ravished child, the infected young man, the spoiled girl. See how hatred and lust throw them one against the other, frozen and seething. See how their hearts turn to stone, rot and decompose. See how, all the while dancing, they become more and more entangled in their own fetters until, in horror, they succumb to the gaping abyss. So goes the world, people say, and they laugh. Who would want to change it? But you do not surrender in defeat. Rather, as if a knife had been plunged into you, you wince with pain and say: "Not like that!" You throw yourselves in the breach. You know that I, your God, have redeemed the world. Through grace you may cast a glance upon my work. Is it perfected? Is sin dead? Is there nothing left for you to accomplish save a bare act of thanksgiving? Has the colossal turning from here to there already been achieved? Is the Kingdom already here? Has the stone been removed? Does not tortured man bellow horribly? You engage yourselves and collapse beneath the wheel. You want to complete in your body what is lacking, what is really lacking, what seems to be lacking of my sufferings.

What then, my children? Preaching? Convincing mankind? When not even my divine Word could affect you? Deeds? The enforcement of Paradise, already here on earth? The infallible Church? The Order of the Awakened? You know where all this leads. You have long been practicing it all: you exert yourselves and bear the scars. And when you look back after long work-filled years, what has been accomplished? Two or three conversions, perhaps even twenty, or a hundred. Where are the others? The work done, the world turned about? Has the deed even begun? Do not the scanty walls, skillfully erected, threaten to cave in again, burying you along with everything else in the rubble? How useless! You raise your eyes and see—perhaps for the first time—the Cross.

In the face of sin's overwhelming power there triumphs only the overwhelming power of grace, from which so much is demanded that it succumbs.

More and more quickly our achievements fall to the ground like outworn husks, and the sweet fruit is revealed around which in the end all else turns: our boundless yearning. With ever greater glow does the wood of creative actions become consumed, until at last only the naked flame of love perdures, and cinderless. Your actions are good, but Paul's chains were better, and all that was left of John in the end was his begging for love. My demand becomes more and more urgent. Nothing satisfies it, nothing is sufficient for it any more. Nothing can close the vacuum that sucks you into itself, or soothe the tears which you see falling or cover over the disgrace on the Face spat upon and crowned with thorns. And so you gather up your soul like a sudarium and raise it up towards me, and because I will be comforted by it, it will henceforth bear my imprint. And, because my image clings to it, the soul also grasps my suffering now, and, by grasping it, joins me in bringing it to completion. I do not spare the soul this sight. There are not two possible sorts of love.

Together, the blood and sweat of our souls run to the ground as one. But you already know what distance lies between us. I bore the entire burden alone, while all the while you slept (when aren't you sleeping?) and your share of the bearing always comes too late—when the Cross has already been suffered through. You do not bear the judgment, but the grace. Even if the burden oppresses you, it nonetheless does so as in a game. My yoke is soft, my burden light. You have received only a hint of the Cross.

Your participation in the redemption (your status as co-redeemers, we might say) is but an analogy, an expression of my love. But it is real: I myself make it real and valid. I make up for your failure and bring it to plenitude. Well then! So, too, should you turn my failure into fullness. Otherwise love would not be love—if I were not to allow you this. Have your share in my failure. Taste with me the futility of the redemption. It is from such stuff that the Father has always wrought his grace. There is a judgment; in the Father's hand there is a balance. In the one scale there lies the heavy and oppressive futility of it all. In the other, a buoyant, mounting hope. And, as the first scale falls, the judgment is decided. Hope mounts up and my Kingdom triumphs; a soaring escape.

CHAPTER XII

THE CONQUEST OF THE BRIDE

M Y KINGDOM IS INVISIBLE, but I want to establish you, my Bride, before the eyes of men so visibly that no one will be able to overlook you. I want to raise you up like the brazen serpent in the desert, like the rock against which hell itself is dashed to pieces, like Mount Tabor over whose peak the shining cloud hovers, and like the Cross that casts its shadow over all lands—the blazon of my victory in failure. I want to establish you upon iron foundations, and your structure is to be a true and distinctive sign that I am setting up a memorial to myself upon the earth. You will be my witness to the very edge of the world, a witness that I was in the world, and I will not forsake you until the end of time. You will be a sign of contradiction among the peoples, and no one will even as much as whisper your name, O my Church, without shuddering. Over you men will have to part their ways, for many will love you and squander everything for you, but very many will hate you, and these will swear an oath not to rest until they have exterminated you from the land of men. And you will be despised like no man or thing, except myself, has ever been despised on earth. They will stand in line for the privilege of spitting in your face, of wiping off on your garments the mud from their shoes. On all walls they will scrawl caricatures of your mystery, and in the bars, writhing with laughter, they will sing obscene songs about you. They will set you in the pillory and, after they have bound and gagged you, they will accuse you of every vulgarity and demand that you wash yourself clean. No means will be left untried to bring you under suspicion and every one of your shortcomings will be inflated to monstrous proportions. You will know hard times, nor will there be any assigned place for you. Wherever the path seemed to lie open before you, you will, before long, find a landslide and a roadblock, or perhaps a wall. "Impossible!", you will say. You will have to live on earth, yet without possessing a home. You will have to acquaint yourself with both the good and the evil customs of every people and with all of men's distresses. But, although you will be in their midst, men will make sure to exclude you from both their trust and their confidence. They will let you feel that you remain the foreigner in the house, at best tolerated, never truly loved. No matter what you may attempt in order to make yourself of service, they will not be satisfied. If you make yourself one of them, they will scorn you; and, if you keep to yourself, they will say: "You see, she knows herself where she belongs. Let's then put an end to the affair and drive her out once and for all." For a time it will seem as though you have attained to well-being and success among them. They will rally around your banner and make themselves at home in the great shadow of your cathedrals. Your word will be their nourishment and your blessing will transfigure their lives. But then it will be as if your children had outgrown the milk of your breasts. The more clever among them will shake themselves loose of your heavenly bonds, and the avalanche of their apostasy will gain momentum through the centuries, until the masses, inexorably dragged along by this irresistible pull towards the earth, will also desert your fold. You who wanted to gather up humanity in order to present it to me as the one fruit in the libation-cup of your prayer: See how you now stand leafless like a tree in the autumn. No harvest has been brought in, and the commandment to go forth which burns within your heart is today still less fulfilled than on the first day when you set out. At that time everything was still possible, even in the midst of the heathen's immense darkness. A light had gone up, and all faces turned automatically towards this New Thing. But now it seems as though your song is becoming a hurdy-gurdy. Whenever you appear in a street all windows are shut, and the little which people's ears nonetheless still unwillingly perceive excites in them nothing but disgust and infinite boredom. You can no longer conceal the disgrace of having failed totally, of having lost the game for good. People's distress may still fill a couple of your bombed-out churches . . . But just wait for the day of prosperity to return and you will be more forgotten than a corpse of a thousand years. You have not recognized the signs of the time. The rushing stream of love that you once released over a thirsty world (the slave raised up a hopeless eye, women lifted their veils, all the disinherited felt the breath of a more-than-earthly mercy): this rushing stream, I say, is now dammed up. Your administrators stingily dole out through well-run pipe-systems and institutions the precious liquid of my grace. The bark of the tree which once blossomed in the wild has now turned to cork. You have become such an established household that even the catastrophic storms of the times, and persecution rattling at your gates and windows, can hardly awaken you from sleep, and a slap in your face can elicit from you but an embarrassed smile. Disgrace covers the length of you, all the more poignantly as you try to deny it, pretending nothing is amiss.

So there you stand, my Bride, truly a sign over the peoples at which fingers point, a widely known but little loved sign. Your failure redounds to me, since on your account my name, too, is blasphemed among the heathen. Many a man who sought me with a sincere heart came to a terrified halt on his way as he suddenly caught sight of you, and he turned away. And many a one who saw how troublesome is the life of your faithful, how little redeemed they appear to be, how pitifully the glow of their hearts smothers under the ashes, how strictly they judge the world while being themselves secretly full of the world; has turned resolutely to the innocence of the heathen. It is not your love—that overcomes the world—which is a scandal to them; for *that* is a scandal which you should give! Their scandal, rather, is your lukewarmness and your unbridled lack of love. You were meant to be for men an image of the unity between me and the Father, and it was for this that I sent you our Holy Spirit, the bond of unifying love; for this it was that I established you on the all-embracing unity of baptism, doctrine, and the uninterrupted succession from Peter to John Paul II. Your very essence is unity, and each of the tokens by which you are recognized and by which you can prove your identity is founded on unity. And you will not succeed in falling away from this unity. You will not succeed because I myself put this unity within you and burnt this indelible mark into you. You will not succeed because I have entered into you with my Spirit and, as your one heart, I move you towards unity from within. But you are always in a state of revolt against yourself. No people is more torn asunder than yours, none so pervaded by discord down to the very foundations. Every person within you who holds an office, everyone who has charge of a mission or who administers a task I have given him, constantly tends to consider the part that he is as if it were the whole. He sees the small wheel he turns as if it were the power that moves everything else, or the worthless service he performs as if it were indispensable. All of you are *members*, and as members all of you should serve so as to complete one another, thankful that your brothers possess what you yourself do not have. In the love which does not seek its own you would possess the whole. For *I* am the whole, I who am the Head of the Body and the soul which unifies it. But no! Down the centuries you quarrel over the better places, forever tearing up and mangling my Body to the bone. And when you do not succeed in tearing a whole member, a whole land, away from the community of the Church, when you, blinded by spite, do not set up a new—the thousandth!—sect alongside my real house, then you strive, insatiable and agitating burrowers that you are, to hollow out like mice the walls *within* the house, and like moles to shake the foundations. Your priests' enviousness has become proverbial, and the fights among your Orders, the rivalries among your organizations, make them the subject of derision. Each individual thinks his own limited program is the best and only valid one, and so the members become detached from one another and my holy, life-giving Blood can no longer flow through them. Long before a new part of your house caves in, long before an external schism is sealed, the sap of love has already become stagnant within; stealthy heresy and omnivorous sin have already made the terrible events inevitable.

It is with you, my Body, that I am forever fighting the great, apocalyptic battle. Whatever remains far from me and my heart is nothing but hollow flesh, lost in itself. But I do not find it difficult to save such flesh: it puts up no resistance and lets itself in due time be brought into the fold. Whoever stands closer to me, however, has been initiated into my mystery and, belonging to my Body, perceives the throbbing of my Heart as it resounds throughout the Body's internal vaulting: *this* person has received the Spirit and is, therefore, awake and able to choose freely. Only *he* truly knows the meaning of sin. Thus, I am endangered within my own Body; it is within me that my deadly enemy lies in wait. I have suckled a snake at my breast, a worm that does not die. In this, too, have I become like you: just as temptation rises within you from your own flesh, so, too, does the deepest threat leap up against me from my own flesh. The spirit is willing and strong, but the flesh is weak, and where the spirit borders on the flesh it is vulnerable, having come to terms with weakness. That is a borderline where the spirit has always betrayed itself, giving itself away. For, if the spirit had nothing of flesh, how could it come to form one being with the flesh? In the same way, I, the strong God, have betrayed myself to you—my Body, my Church—and in the place where I did this I became weak: there alone could I be wounded to the death. In that place I yielded, I surrendered to the temptation of loving a body within my own Body (for who can hate his own flesh?); the temptation of delivering myself up to the obscure chaos of a body, of plunging below the shiny surface of the flesh; the temptation of passing over into this world—this simmering darkness, opposed to the Father's light; the temptation, I say, of

passing over into this adventure of the senses, into
this unknown virgin forest called Mankind. Just as
you, passionately, with throbbing pulse, cross over
temptation's boundary, so, too, have I crossed over
the boundary of the flesh with a quivering heart, fully
conscious of the danger. I dared to enter the body of
my Church, the deadly body which *you* are. For the
spirit is mortal only within its own body. And so,
from now on, we are no longer two but, together,
only one flesh which loves itself and which struggles
and wages battle with itself even to the point of death.
For your sake I became weak, since I could experience your being only in weakness. No wonder you
realized your advantage over me and took my nakedness by storm! But I have defeated you through
weakness and my Spirit has overpowered my unruly
and recalcitrant flesh. (Never has woman made more
desperate resistance!) In order to put a seal on my victory and exploit my triumph, I have engraved a mark
upon you, O my flesh: on your carnal weakness I
have engraved the mark of my own carnal weakness,
and on your sin the mark of my love. Never again
will your sinful battle against me be anything other
than the long wrestling of love. This is the meaning I
confer upon it, and now it can have no other meaning. Precisely because you, O wretched one, know-
ingly sin against love, precisely for that reason is your
sin enfolded by my love. And because I, who am at
once Spirit and Love, am myself the battlefield between God and the world, the battle is already and

eternally won in me. Our wrecked covenant—our blood-wedding, the red wedding of the Lamb—is already, here and now, the white bridal bed of divine love.

Do what you will, you remain the captive of love. I raised you up, wild one, when you were struggling and weltering in your own blood. I have washed you in the bath of my Blood, in the water-bath of my baptism and in the Word of Life, and I have fashioned for myself a glorious Church, without blemish or wrinkle, holy and unspotted. You may behave like a wanton courtesan and daily betray me with another: still, you will never be what you in this way pretend to be. For all eternity you are my pure Body and my chaste Spouse. I am going to clothe your disgrace with such holiness that the aroma of your garments will fill the whole earth, and no one will be able to deny that he has really and bodily sensed your fragrance. I will deposit such love into your hands—love for you to distribute—that your name among the peoples will be called "The Lovable" and "Love's Watchtower." And I will put in your heart such concern for the world and for my lost sheep that the dull herd will smell their shepherd and run to you almost against their will. The insults which you are preparing for me will not be as great as the disgrace that I will bestow upon you from the treasury of my Cross. The mockery they will pile upon you will be nothing compared with the mockery I will entrust to you as my precious gift and my priceless wedding present, taken from the storehouse of my divine sufferings. The inglorious weakness with which, in this century of collapse, you stand before the world unable to transform it: this weakness is already a part of the mystery of my own inglorious weakness, for when was *I* ever strong enough to renew the face of this exterior world? Thus, it is my will to give you a worth which does not properly belong to you, and to fashion you solely from the might of my heart, as Eve was fashioned from Adam's rib.

The source of your life, O Church, is both a demand and a promise. Live not from yourself; live solely in me and from me. Think of yourself no longer as of the one you used to be. Think no longer of your heart, but rather let my Heart alone be sufficient for you—the heart which I have planted in the center of your body. You ought, in this way, to be my Bride and my Body, and it is my will to redeem the whole world in you, exclusively in you. Be my handmaid. Renounce your will and nestle, like Ruth, at my feet. Become obedient even to death. Be for the world my embodied obedience, shown forth visibly and sensibly throughout all ages. Be so obedient that to say "Church" will be to say "obedience"; for redemption is found in obedience, and whoever proclaims me must depict my obedience even to the death on the cross. Thus it is that I want to exalt you to be Queen of the World, and all peoples and ages will have to bow before you. You, however, yourself obeying, are to exact obedience in my name, for it is my will to

rule the world in none other than you, and in no
other body but yours does my Heart throb. This is
the demand and this the promise. Bind yourself to me
so irrevocably that I will be able to descend to hell
with you; and then I will bind you to myself so irrevocably that, with me, you will be able to ascend to
very heaven. Empty yourself out into me so com-
pletely that I can fill you with myself. I will spare you
no extremity—not the heights and not the depths—
for I wish to have no secret from you. Where I am,
there you too are to be. What I do, that are you to do
in me. So it is that I wish to teach you my obedience:
a blind obedience leading you to abandon your every
insight, your every love, your every faith, and
through this obedience they will recognize who has
my Spirit and who belongs to my Body. But this
obedience will be but the pledge of my love for you
and of your love for me, and in the midst of your
slavish service you will experience the freedom of the
children of God coming upon you like the ray of a
light from above. You will experience how greatly
servitude follows the coercion of love. In all of this
you will fare as I did when I, by being my Father's
slave, was only bound the more intimately to his
love, and every creaturely distance from my Father
revealed itself as a means and a detour and a more
cunning ruse leading towards unification. I now repeat with you the same game which the Father played
with me. I dismiss you, out into the world; I leave
you behind on earth, widowed, only in order to unite

myself to you from heaven in a more interior, more spiritual, more divine manner. I leave you as if bereft of soul in the grave of the world, with your spirit wandering among the shades of the underworld, only to deliver you from death suddenly, abruptly, thus again proving to the world that you live and that I live in you. For your existence in the world is an incessant miracle, and no one can ignore the fact that you drink from an alien spring, that a table other than theirs nourishes you. And so, in spite of everything, you *will* be my sign among the nations. To them you will remain a very implausible thing, so much so that they will daily prophesy your death. And you will indeed die after a fashion. But see: we live, you and I, for I have died once and whoever eats of my death will live eternally and I will awaken him on the Last Day—and each day is the last. I have died once, and only once does my Body, my Church, pass over from death to life. This is the one turning. Each of your members must make it a reality in union with me, each in his own place, in his own century, but in the unity of the one change, in the transubstantiation of this world into the other world (they are the same). There is but one turning wherein earth becomes heaven, and this turning point is the Church. Here the occluded world opens up and awaits the promised grace. Here man confesses his guilt and recognizes his truth. By the very act of becoming exposed, man's truth is effaced and in its place he receives the truth of God. Here the old man is replaced by the new. Here the world dies and another world rises. Here the two eons intersect. Here every ending becomes a beginning, every impasse becomes the pledge of a hope. Here springs forth out of the hardest rock the water of eternal life. Here ends the road of reason and faith sprouts wings. Here the puzzle of the world is solved through the mystery of God. Here is bridged the chasm between heaven and earth, because your faithful live in both realms at once. Blessedness is no longer a distant promise: this, rather, is eternal life— that in love they have come to know you, Father, and also me, whom you have sent. And no human flinching concerning salvation will constitute such shaky ground that the Rock of Faith will not outdo instability with firmness. "For my sheep hear my voice, and I know them, and they follow after me, and I give them eternal life, and they will not in all eternity be lost, and no one will snatch them from my hand. My Father, who has given them to me, is greater than all others, and no one can steal from the Father's hand. I and the Father are one." This is why I myself am the Resurrection and the Life, and whoever believes in me, whoever drinks from the source that flows from my open side, from *him* a new source will spring forth which will be inexhaustible, for it flows from eternal life into eternal life. And, Martha, it will not be on the Last Day that I will awaken him, for whoever believes in me has already passed over from death to life. His grave has already burst open and he has risen to eternal life. This is eternal life, that believing, loving and hoping, they come to know you, Father, and also me, whom you have sent.

To you, my Church, have I entrusted this fountainhead. Out of you, who are my Body, out of your open side does it flow forth to refresh all peoples. Just as you, as the new Eve, have sprung forth from my sleep, so do I, who am divine life itself, spring forth from you. Your hands distribute me as the Bread of the World. For, to be sure, the woman derives from the man, but the man is then born of the woman. Everything, however, derives from God. Being God, I am the Source and am before every being, and for this reason the man is the glory of God and the source of the woman, and God-become-human is the man, while the Church is a woman, since the woman is the glory of the man. But, because I became the Son of Man, I have been born from human beings and am your child, O Church. For everyone who does the will of my Father is not only my brother and my sister, but my mother as well. You have sprung forth from my Heart and I have rested under your heart. You, to whom I gave birth with much suffering at the Cross, will be prostrate in painful labor with me until the end of the world. Your image mysteriously blurs to merge with the image of my virginal Mother. She is an individual woman, but in you she becomes the cosmic Mother. For in you my individual Heart, too, widens to become the Heart of the World. You yourself are the holy heart of the nations, holy because of me, but unifying the world for me, making my Blood circulate throughout the body of history. In you my redemption ripens, I myself grow to my full stature, until I, two-in-one with you, and in the bond of the two-in-one flesh—you, my Bride and my Body—will place at the feet of the Father the Kingdom which we are. The bond of our love is the meaning of the world. In it all things reach fulfillment. For the meaning of the world is love.

CHAPTER XIII

LOVE—A WILDERNESS

O THE BLESSED WILDERNESS that is your love! No one will ever be able to subdue you, no one explore you. The roads they rashly began to lay do not penetrate very far. They suddenly break off and the disillusionment of the pioneers still floats in the air. You can detect their mood as they have to turn around. Other paths have again grown over. The grass of the virgin forest presses in from both sides. Tall trunks have fallen across them. Again the wilderness hums and blossoms, boundless.

When I was still young I thought one could come into the clear with you. I saw a steep road ahead of me and I felt my courage swell. So I fastened my knapsack and began to climb. I attempted to make myself light by following your word and forsaking all things in spirit. For a time it even seemed to me I was rising higher. But today, after all these years, when I lift up my eyes, I see your dazzling pinnacles towering over me higher and more unreachable than ever. And I have long since stopped talking about a road.

I had fully equipped myself with regional maps and measuring devices. I knew the twelve steps of humility by heart, as well as the seven ramparts and moats drawn around the fortress of the soul. On many a mountain peak I saw little flags and signals set up, and on the boulders red and blue markings let me know that many a climber had already gone by there. Certain camping spots were littered with "Instructions for the Blessed Life" as if with tinfoil or empty cans of sardines. As time went on I lost the habit of paying any attention to these familiar remains. It only struck me that they became more and more sparse, and they appeared to be old and rusty and on the verge of becoming a part of the wilderness themselves, lost as they were in the thicket of the virgin forest and in the tangle of branches.

And all those who tried to domesticate you and rob you of your magic seemed to me to be childish and silly. And I felt anger towards them rising up in me because they were misleading the souls of those who could have grasped your magic, O my wilderness. But compassion also came over me, because they were cheating the world and themselves out of the best of all goods. And one day I threw everything in the bushes—knapsack, provisions and map—and I consecrated myself to you alone, O virginal landscape, and I became free for you.

The teachers said: the Ways of Knowledge are three. The Way of the Yes, the Way of the No, and, more sublime than either, the Way of the Ultimate Beyond. The first would have me find you in all creatures, since each of them reflects as in a fragment a ray of your light. The second would have me forsake all creatures, since their hard contours cannot contain your infinitely flowing Being. The third way would, finally, have me smash the shell of their perfections and dilate them until they become the measureless measure of your eternity. But I learned that these ways are no way at all. The Yes is a dictum, and the No a contra-diction. They become entangled with each other, and in the end they both lead to the abyss, while the third way is but the impossibility of crossing it. Many advise: "Throw yourself into the depths so that your own being and limits will shatter, and thus you will find what you so long for. Your eyes will be opened and you will be like God."

Such reasoning contained a great temptation, and from the depths of the crater golden lava, divine life itself seemed to beckon enticingly. Gold from this gold seemed to me the light which (tradition has it) at times would beam out in the night for distant seafarers from the highest cliffs of Mount Athos. And that ecstasy seemed to me holy which made it possible for Plotinus and Al-Halladj and the disciples of the Bodhisattva to soar above all limitation.

But at just the right moment I remembered your Heart, Lord, and I recalled that you have loved your creatures' limitations and that you descended into our earthly valley to dwell here among us until the end of the world and to warn us against the spirit's seductiveness and against showing contempt for even the least of these little ones. And as I looked at you and saw you sitting exhausted at the whore's well, saw you smearing mud and spittle on the eyes of the man born blind, the suspicion began to grow in me that the only thing those *illuminati* had encountered in their ecstasies was the masked phantom of their own hollow nostalgia. And thus, those others also must have been deluding themselves who pretended to know of a way that bypassed your humanity and went beyond it, so as to arrive at what they claimed is the Father's more profound "groundlessness."

The truth of it was that every way which was not yourself failed. All those who did not know you went astray, and only those knew you who were in you. Not even the distance from me to you was passable if it had not been trod in advance in you.

But you yourself, Lord: how are you a way? You are unlike any human road. None of your words is a sure indicator of the next, in the way in which milestones show distance and a clear direction. Every direction is a judgment and an execution; every execution of a plan is a prosecution; every prescription a proscription. The Way that you are—and you ARE a way—should remove every solid road from beneath our feet. Every step forward at once pushes us back into the greater gulf of our nothingness and it shoves us to the side that, kneeling in the dust, we may open the way for you to advance alone—you who are the King of Glory. We are to do works and to grow through works, but in growing we are to become smaller and in looking on you we are to forget all our works. Our righteousness ought to be greater than that of the scribes and Pharisees, but we ought to become smaller and more lowly than this child. We are to store up treasures in heaven, and in solid barns where rust and moths won't consume them; but we are also to be the poorest of men and blessed beggars in spirit, not worrying fearfully about the morrow—the Eternal Day. With great in-tensity we ought to run after what lies before us, and yet we ought to rest, in careless dis-tension, like a bird in your hand. Our works should shine before men, but we should take care to perform them in secret. We are to be perfect as our Father in heaven, but also crushed in spirit, like the publican in the temple, experiencing ourselves as good-for-nothing sinners. We are to be watchful, mature, and, as your friends, initiated into the full depth of your mysteries; but as your servants we ought not desire to know either the day or the hour. We are to exert ourselves for men and die for them like women in labor. And yet, when they don't receive us, we are simply to keep walking after shaking the dust from our feet. We ought to be even-tempered and desirous of no gift, but at the same time empathetic both in sorrow and in joy and open-handed, both in giving and in receiving. Patient as a seed, we are to let your Kingdom grow in us, like a sown field rising steadily and full of weeds; but, bold as lightning, we are to snatch the Kingdom of Heaven to ourselves with violence in the flash of the great decision.

Where is there a way here? Where any kind of indication? Is this not the wilderness? And who can grasp your Kingdom? Your Kingdom is small as a mustard seed and yet surpasses all other seeds in growth. It is commingled of the good and the worthless and yet admits no one who is evil. It is distant and not of this world and has nevertheless come close to us to dwell among us. It draws near us when we are far-off and sit in the shadow of death and yet escapes us when we approach it and try to encompass it . . . This Kingdom—your presence in the world—is as ungraspable as you are yourself. For it is all things at once: it is poor and rich, mighty and powerless, so visible that no one can overlook it with impunity, and yet so secret that no one can perceive it without the eyes of grace. In the Sacraments, the love of God lays itself at our feet almost in the manner of a slave, binding itself to its own irrevocable decision to become tangible and available in water and bread and wine and oil. But if someone should snatch out at God's love so as to catch it, it will slip through his grasping fingers like the wind, that derides all barbed enclosures. And you, O Church, princess and queen over all peoples, inviolably established at the Ruler's right hand, Bride without stain or wrinkle, but also greying old-maid and rejected hussy, almost to be mistaken for red Babylon sitting on the back of the beast! And you, Christians, luminaries of the world and lights upon the bushel-basket, salt of the nations and freedmen of God, but also a scandal before men, despised for your sins and persecuted with good reason and not for Christ's sake! Citizens of heaven, disenfranchised from this world, yet having to exert yourselves with great effort day after day, dragging yourselves from confession to confession: Who are you?

Wilderness, also, in the hearts that willingly resist, that nostalgically fence themselves in, that yield in retreat even as they press forward. Wilderness in men's consciences, which are evil and yet again good, full of the certainty of being God's children and moaning with uncertainty as to whether they deserve wrath or love. Wilderness of love itself, that does not know whether it really loves, since perhaps even now, under so many roses of self-surrender, it may in fact be nothing but rank concupiscence: love that may be nothing but a fractured, crumbling ruin even as it is more certain of the gift of God's outpoured love in its heart and of the solid edifice built upon Christ the Lord.

Wilderness, finally, that is this great, intricate tangle of a world: stiff rock and foaming wave; the eternal return of the same and constant transformation into things that have never been before; order in the path of the stars and the thronging of atoms . . . Yet does not the world constantly overflow every conceivable law with enigmatic freedom? The world is entrusted to man as a garden for him to cultivate and bring to never-ending progress. And yet the world is a careless chaos which ever anew spills over every enclosure, breaking tips which have been overly sharpened, forcing rising curves to descend as if by nature, making overripe forms return to the primal womb. It is a world in which meaning and counter-meaning keep each other in equilibrium and in which every part calls for a counterpart. It is a world which rounds itself off into an egg and compresses all impulses towards the heavens within its own atmosphere, and also a world which yet lies there open beyond all closing, like a dissected body, its entrails groaning for a fullness which it can never give to itself. With straining fingers the world points to God, and with every fiber of its body it thirsts for him as for the most urgently needed rain. All possible forces rise up from the depths of this world, and yet it cowers in impotence and anxiously waits for grace to descend. Equivocal world, whose bi-unity and disunity is the most univocal thing about it! Middle-world, which yet brings Creator and creature into unity precisely by keeping them apart! Monster-world, that rears its head and swallows up God himself in human form. Child-world, that in the end is a suckling infant dreaming in the arms of the Virgin Mary . . .

Who can grasp the Lord's meaning in his creation and beyond it? Who can tie up with a short string the unbounded bouquet of wisdom? Who can tame the jungle of his incomprehensibility? See how man's spirit and whole being lies, like the bowl of an impetuous fountain, under the downpour of so many mysteries. Let it gush! By letting it gush you will grasp what you can, and what you can is to be a bowl for the flood. Open up heart and brain and do not attempt to clutch tightly. By being washed out you will become purified. The strange thing that flows through you is precisely the meaning you seek. The more you give away through renunciation, the richer your wisdom becomes. The more you receive by holding out your hands, the stronger your power becomes. See: Everything wants to bewilder you so that, out of the abundance of bewilderment, you will know the superabundance of love. Everything wants to empty you out, so that you become a hollow space for the superabundance of faith. Everything wears you through like a cloth so that, by becoming threadbare through constant friction, you will be transparent to the superabundance of light.

For look: everything, down to the last atom, is dissolved into its elements and transported, then to crystallize anew around the one crystal of the absolute Center. Everything must die in the death throes of unknowing, for it is only out of the material of perfect impotency that the royal garment of the World Conqueror can be woven. Everything must enter this current, like icefloes that crack open under the sun with a roar and lose their own shape and roll out to the sea in a mighty tumble. But this movement is produced by the heartbeat at the Center, and what appeared to be a chaotic impulse is the blood circulating in the Body of the cosmic Christ.

This is the body in which you are to flow, letting yourself be driven ever anew as a drop through red ventricles and throbbing arteries. In this circulation you will experience both the futility of your resistance as you put up a struggle and the power of the muscle that drives you forward. You will experience the anguish of the creature that must humble and lose itself, but also the sheer joy of the divine life, which consists in being a closed circuit of endlessly flowing love. Washed along on the tide of the sacred Blood, you will encounter all things as pebble knocks against pebble in the cataracts of a mountain stream, but also in the way handsome sailboats cross on the gently changing landscape of a royal river. Pushed along in the detachment of dark solitude, you will learn to know that the communion of all beings among themselves is their contact with one another and their selfhood within the flowing channels of that Body. Thus related to all things and all natures, you will at last be able to commune also with yourself, and by way of self-forgetfulness—that lengthiest of all detours—you will be brought to the festive Table of Offerings upon which you will find yourself lying as a stranger who is given to himself as a new gift. Expelled from the Heart, out to all the members of that colossal Body, you will undertake a voyage longer than any of Columbus'. But just as the earth rounds itself off into a ball, so, too, do the veins make a return to the Heart and love goes out and comes back eternally. Slowly you will master the rhythm, and you will no longer grow fearful when the Heart drives you out into emptiness and death, for then you will know that that is the shortest route to be admitted again into fullness of delight. And when it pushes you away from itself, then you should know that this is your mission: being sent away from the Son, you yourself repeat the way of the Son, away from the Father and out to the world. And your way to remote places, where the Father is not, is the way of God himself, who goes out from himself, abandons himself, lets himself fall, leaves himself in the lurch. But this going out of the Son is also the going out of the Spirit from the Father and the Son, and the Spirit is the return of the Son to the Father. At the outermost margin of existence, at the furthest shore, where the Father is invisible and wholly hidden, there the Son breathes out his Spirit, whispers it into the chaos and the darkness, and the Spirit of God hovers over the waters. And hovering in the Spirit, the Son turns back to the Father glorified, and you along with him and in him, and the departure and the return are one and the same. Nothing any longer exists outside of this one and only flowing life.

HOW I THANK YOU, LORD, that I am allowed to flow and do not have to grasp, am allowed to expand out into your blessed incomprehensibility and do not have to puzzle anxiously over signs and written formulas. For everything is a hieroglyph but it tells of you, and everything is a sign and points to you. And over the universal riddle your mystery dawns like a sun, and in the decline of all worldly light your greater light glimmers in silence. Every road pushes me violently out of myself and into the wilderness, and no longer finding any road I can sense your wing and your breath. How I thank you, Lord, that you transcend our heart, for at last everything we can comprehend lies pitifully beneath us. And our spirit does not desire to contain, but to be contained in you, and even in knowing, rather to be known by your Heart. When all wisdom collapses, it is not unknowing that we experience, but rather the truth that all wisdom is secured in you. The wave of the world boils up boldly, but then its impetus overshoots itself and turns to spray, and it casts itself, widely dispersed, upon your shore in spent adoration. How I thank you, Lord, that you resolve the painful wilderness of the world only by dissolving it into the blessed wilderness of your love, and that everything conflicting and raging within us is melted together in the crucible of your creator's might. I thank you that everything in us which is ambiguous and which, therefore, gleams seductively, is reconciled in you and beams with the redemption that makes two into one. You transfigure enigma and replace it with mystery. Everything, sin included, is to you raw material and building stones. Through your atonement you take each being to yourself and, without destroying its reality, you confer upon it a new being. You change refuse into jewels, coquetry into virginalness, and on the hopeless you bestow a future. Your sorcerer's hand outdoes all of childhood's fairy-tales. At all moments you are the living fountain of all possibilities, and the real yields and is molded in your fingers with all the ease of clay on the potter's wheel. You are more fantastic than any dream, and our most extravagant utopias are but a poor and dull imitation of what you have long ago brought into reality. Indeed, your inventions and free imaginings are the most intimate dream of all things, one which they hardly dared dream, one they were incapable of dreaming. But once you take them in your mouth and pronounce them as you see fit, then you have enunciated their very being, and they are given as gifts to themselves. How I thank you, Lord, that my being transcends me to pass out into you, and that my center lies beyond myself in you. Whether I like it or not, and in spite of all resistance, I must, so to speak, be derailed from the crooked track of my heart to cross over into you. And thus, all things open up to you like eggs out of which young life emerges, like buds that burst, and all beings lean out of their windows straining towards you, and in you, beyond themselves, they find both you and themselves. They fall into place around you like a flower's petals around the hidden pistil, whose taciturn presence becomes manifest only as a fragrance.

The Rose of the World loses its petals, all of us wither and decline, but in such an autumn your springtime blossoms. Like fallow foliage we fall away, drift aimlessly, turn to mould and decay. What comes from the earth turns into earth: the earthly-minded heart. And then again the heavenly garden turns into a rampant wilderness. We are not God. The silence at this boundary is not to be penetrated. To be bounded is our very form; boundary is our destiny and our happiness. We may not shatter our shape: you yourself show respect before this our shape. We step back into distance. Love is found only in distance, unity only in difference. God himself is unity of Spirit only in the distinction of Father and Son. That we stand over against you and are receptive mirrors is in us the seal of your authorship. We are like you by not being you. We share in the nearness of love by being pushed back into the remoteness of awe. For love is chaste, and God's bosom is virginal. And the Queen, your Mother, is virgin and maiden.

We fall down and adore you. In the end, only you remain, O Heart at the Center! We *are* not. Whatever is good in us is you. What we ourselves are is negligible. We pass by before you and aspire to be nothing more than mirrors and windows for our brothers. Our setting before you is your rising over us: our merging into you and your entry into us. For still does our decline before you bear the figure of your own decline, and still does our guilty distance from you belong not to ourselves, since you have made it into a distance of your own, Sin has the form of redemption.

And so in the end you remain alone, all in all. You are one with yourself, and without losing yourself you pour yourself out into the many. By remaining in the multiplicity of the members, you bring them all home into the unity of the Body. Your self-emptying, even unto uttermost weakness and the renouncing of love, is your deed of uttermost strength and immutable love, and when you are weakest and they all trample you like a worm, it is then you are the Hero and have trampled the serpent. For what is emptiness? What fullness? Which of them is real privation? When you are empty and thirst for fullness, then we, the Church, are your fulfillment. And when you are full and, like a wet-nurse, you long to unburden your teeming and aching breast, then, too, are we, the Church, your fulfillment. But you are always the fullness and we are the void, always; even when you are fatigued and spent with exhaustion, even then do we all receive from your fullness grace upon grace. Your Church is but a vessel, she is only your organ. You are the leaping fountain. And even if out of us also there springs up a stream into life everlasting, this is a draft which you gave, for only from you do streams of living water flow. And when you go through the world poor and gray, cloaked in the garments of the lowly and the disinherited, concealing yourself behind sinners and tax-collectors, and we absent-mindedly perform on you the eight works of mercy, even then you alone are the giver who has made love possible for us from both within and without.

You alone remain. You are all in all. Even if your love desires us in order to delight in twoness and in order to celebrate with us the mystery of begetting and conceiving, nevertheless it is always YOUR love in both instances, your love which both gives and is given, at once seed and womb, and, again, the child

218

begotten is none other than you. If love needs two feet in order to walk, still the walker is but one person, and that one is you. And if love needs two lovers, a lover and a beloved, still the love is only one, and that one is you.

Everything hearkens back to your throbbing Heart. Time and the seasons still hammer away and create, and your Heart drives the world and all its happenings forward with great painful blows. It is the unrest of the clock, and your Heart is restless until it rests in me. Your Heart is restless until we rest in you, once time and eternity have become interfused. But: Be at peace! I have overcome the world. The torment of sin has already been submerged in the stillness of love. The experience of what the world is has made love darker, more fiery, more ardent. The shallower abyss of rebellion has been swallowed up in unfathomable mercy, and throbbing majestically reigns serene the Heart of God.